PRAISE FOR *THE JOY OF MISSING OUT*

"If you've ever said 'yes' to an obligation when you really wanted to say 'no,' read this book. If you've ever felt like your to-do list is longer at the end of the day despite your best efforts, read this book. If you've ever wished there was a twenty-fifth hour in the day, read this book. If you're ready for more joy and less fear, read this book."

—JON ACUFF, *New York Times* bestselling author
of *Finish: Give Yourself the Gift of Done*

"In a world that continually tells you to do more, this book gives you permission to do less. Tonya shares why 'missing out' is exactly the right choice to make and encourages you to live a life aligned with what's important!"

—LEENA RINNE, vice president of Consulting
at Franklin Covey Company

"We all have dreams and desires to live a life of great relationships, meaningful work, and purpose. Yet the demands of time, the needs of others, and our own expectations of who we should be, overwhelm us and muddy the waters. Tonya Dalton's thoughtful system to get back in control of your life is workable and simple. She helps you become focused on the truly significant and gives you the courage to prune back those to-do's that are holding you back from the person you were made to be."

—JOHN TOWNSEND, *New York Times* bestselling
author of *Boundaries* and *People Fuel*

"One of the biggest challenges we face today is overwhelm and a constant feeling of being busy. Tonya Dalton's *The Joy of Missing Out* is the antidote we have been waiting for—empowering us through productivity to live our best lives."

—JOHN O'LEARY, bestselling author of *On Fire*
and host of the *Live Inspired* podcast

"*The Joy of Missing Out* will give you permission to want what you really want and to chase after it without apology. I can't think of a better, more experienced, or more productive person to learn this from than Tonya Dalton—the champion of JOMO."

—LINDSAY TEAGUE MORENO, entrepreneur,
speaker and author of *Boss Up!*

"Many things in life are worth missing out on. This book is not one of them. Pick this book up if you want to discover what your deepest-held priorities should be, get to know yourself better than you have before, and actually act on what's important every day. I loved this book and couldn't put it down."

—**CHRIS BAILEY**, author of *Hyperfocus* and *The Productivity Project*

"Feeling effective is more satisfying than feeling busy. In this gentle and encouraging book, Tonya shows you how to focus your mind and your time on what matters and how to stop worrying about everything else."

—**LAURA VANDERKAM**, author of *I Know How She Does It: How Successful Women Make the Most of Their Time*

"*The Joy of Missing Out* didn't tell me to be less ambitious and slow down, instead it gave me the tools I needed to have purpose and clarity about my to-do lists. Tonya helps you take all the pieces floating around in your life and be intentional about them. If the words *busy* and *overwhelmed* frequent your vocabulary, do yourself a favor and read *The Joy of Missing Out*."

—**JESS EKSTROM**, founder of Headbands of Hope and author of *Chasing the Bright Side*

"Tonya is like the fairy godmother of productivity for the modern woman. In a world where we feel pressure to do it all but end up empty inside and achieving nothing at all, Tonya swoops in with a fresh message that gives women permission to get off the hamster wheel. Instead of doing everything, she gives us a practical and inspirational guide on how to reconnect with what truly matters most, how to architect the lives we desire on our own terms, and how to establish bliss in the middle of our messy, busy lives."

—**MARSHAWN EVANS DANIELS**, Godfidence coach, TV personality, reinvention strategist for Women, and founder of SheProfits.com

"In this important and necessary book, Tonya Dalton gives us the greatest gift we could ask for: permission to be ourselves by relieving us of the pressure to be anyone else. *The Joy of Missing Out* will allow you to rediscover what really matters to you—and help you say no to the things that don't."

—**JEFF GOINS**, bestselling author of *The Art of Work*

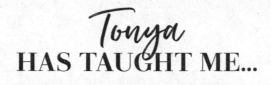

Tonya
HAS TAUGHT ME...

That my ideal day can become my everyday. To be *intentional* with my time and *energy* so I can focus on my goals and *dreams*. She has taught me life does not have to be busy to be productive and *fulfilling*. Sarah B, Greenhouse Manager & Knitwear Designer ⬡ How to *prioritize* and how to stop living a life where I can only chase fires but instead realize I deserve better and can do *better*. Carrie L, Project Manager ⬡ The *tools* to living each day with *purpose*. Tina F, Professor & CEO of My Family ⬡ To be patient with myself, give myself grace, and recognize the *"Joy of Missing Out."* Jacquei S, Palliative Care CNS ⬡ New *frameworks* for creating systems that support productivity and intentionality. Gail H, Leadership Coach ⬡ How to *prioritize* my time based on what is *important* to me. Brittany E, Assistant Director of Advising ⬡ To set my own priorities and find time for them. Meredith C, Civil Servant ⬡ Important *values* and beliefs to carry *forward* into whatever comes into this new phase of my life. I treasure every nugget of wisdom she shares and her *generous* spirit goes *beyond* words! I am forever *grateful!* Deb W, Administrative Assistant, Artist at Heart ⬡ To stop striving for a life where everything is perfect. How to *dig deep* and get to the *heart* of what I truly want. Julie ZY, App Developer ⬡ How to use my North Star to guide the choices I make. She has helped me to *reconnect* to what's most *important* to me and to use that *clarity* to cut through the overwhelm. Michelle D, Program Director at a Non-Profit ⬡ How to be *mission driven* in all aspects of my life, not just in my work life. Debra S, Professor ⬡ Not only how to self reflect but how to take that self *reflection* and turn it into *actionable* goals! She taught me *intentionality* which is such a gift and life changing! Nichole M, Audit and Consulting Professional ⬡ The importance in finding the right accountability partner. Mariana B, Wealth Management Associate ⬡ A *structure* and a vocabulary to reclaim my *goals* and my *vision* for my life. Amy B, Professional Development Manager ⬡ How to prioritize my day and *focus* on my goals. Susan J, Educator ⬡ To find my lane and run in it for all it's worth. Laura H, Instructional Technologist ⬡ How to bring *clarity* to my life. Liz M, Financial Office Manager ⬡ It's ok to *say no* and to put yourself first. It's ok to *prioritize* those things that are *important* to you and *focus* on the things *you* want to focus on. Chris W, Human Resources Business Partner ⬡ That it is possible to create and live your *ideal* life. Leah H, Pharmaceutical Process Engineer ⬡ How to *actuate* my biggest, scariest goal that is solely for me. Taska S, Owner of Naturalist Studio ⬡ Being *overwhelmed* just means you need a place to start and then she showed me how to organize all my to-do's to find my *starting point* and take off. Brenda C, Senior Business Analyst for Software Company ⬡ How to clarify my ideas to get a *clearer* picture of my *goals*. Sarah Mc, Wife, Mother, & Chaos Coordinator ⬡ To have *harmony* in my life. Dionne M, Business Owner ⬡ To live with *intention*. Kristi C, Program Director for Software Company ⬡ That *productivity* is not about doing more, it's about getting the important things done. Amy K, Assistant Dean

Testimonials from *real* women, like you, who have worked
through the four steps covered in this book.

THE JOY OF
missing out

LIVE MORE BY DOING LESS

TONYA DALTON

NELSON
BOOKS
An Imprint of Thomas Nelson

Published in Nashville, Tennessee, by Nelson Books, an imprint of Thomas Nelson. Nelson Books and Thomas Nelson are registered trademarks of HarperCollins Christian Publishing, Inc.

Published in association with Yates & Yates, www.yates2.com.

Thomas Nelson titles may be purchased in bulk for educational, business, fund-raising, or sales promotional use. For information, please email SpecialMarkets@ThomasNelson.com.

Any internet addresses, phone numbers, or company or product information printed in this book are offered as a resource and are not intended in any way to be or to imply an endorsement by Thomas Nelson, nor does Thomas Nelson vouch for the existence, content, or services of these sites, phone numbers, companies, or products beyond the life of this book.

All interviews and personal stories are used with permission.

ISBN 978-1-4002-1425-8 (eBook)
ISBN 978-1-4002-1433-4 (HC)
ISBN 978-1-4002-1943-8 (custom)

Library of Congress Control Number: 2019946663

Printed in the United States of America
19 20 21 22 23 LSC 10 9 8 7 6 5 4 3 2 1

To John, Jack, and Kate: true joy can be found in the moments I spend with you.

JOY OF MISSING OUT

Also Known As: JOMO

Noun

1. The emotionally intelligent antidote to busy; intentionally choosing to live in the present moment by embracing open spaces of unrushed time

   Example: *She wanted more Joy of Missing Out in her life, so she intentionally left her computer in her office, eliminating the temptation to check in with work during family time.*

2. An intense feeling of delight and happiness caused by centering your life on what is truly important and letting go of the "shoulds" and "have tos" in life

   Example: *She decided not to be weighted down by social pressure and chose to find the Joy of Missing Out by saying no to accepting another board position out of guilt.*

SYNONYMS: unhurried purpose, intentional, priority-centered
ANTONYMS: busy, hustle, frazzled, knock stuff out, having a full plate

CONTENTS

OVERWHELMED.

It was a beautiful spring morning, but I was too busy to notice the trees beginning to bud or the clear blue sky. I was on a mission. I had already run the elementary school gauntlet known as carpool and was doing my best to keep it all together as I raced the clock, trying to get Kate to preschool drop-off in time. I hustled her inside the narrow hallways, barely avoiding the still-wet, two-day-old finger paintings lining the walls.

Together we hung up her backpack, and she took out her lunch bag while I counted to ten in my head, trying not to feel the impatience crawling up my skin. I was anxious. I had a busy day ahead, and I had a to-do list three miles long to prove it. With a quick kiss on Kate's cheek and a wave to her teacher, I raced back down the hallway, doing my best to avoid any conversations or chances of being roped into another committee.

Finally I opened my car door and sank into the driver's seat, ready to start my day. I remember rushing home and standing in the middle of my bright yellow kitchen, mentally running through all the tasks I needed to do.

I took a step toward my laundry room and stopped. *No, not laundry.* I took a step toward my computer and shook my head. *No, I shouldn't work on that yet.* I turned around and around again and again as I debated what to do first. I was spinning like a top in slow motion; I literally turned in a circle. The feeling of overwhelm was bubbling up inside of me, making me feel light-headed and just-this-side of crazy. I crumpled into a heap on the floor and cried for a good fifteen minutes.

When I pulled myself up, still breathing ragged breaths, I was angry at myself. *How could I have wasted time crying when I had so much to do?* I used my sleeve to roughly wipe away the salt from my cheeks, said a few choice words to myself about how weak I was, and moved on with my day. I buried those emotions deep inside. After all, I had a to-do list to tackle.

———

This is a true story. Though I didn't know it at the time, I was the cause of my own overwhelm. I was busy simply being "busy"—filling my day with errands and tasks but never feeling like I'd done enough. It made me feel like I was running in circles, leaving me exhausted and irritable. I was busy doing "all the things" so other women would look at me and think I had it all together. But I didn't. Most days started with me wondering how I would possibly keep up this facade and ended with me feeling like a failure.

I was living my days in this constant state of overwhelm.

Overwhelmed.

This is the word I hear from so many women when they describe how they feel about their days. It doesn't seem to matter how old they are, what season of life they're in, or what job they do. *Overwhelm* is the thread that connects each of them.

Overwhelmed by their responsibilities. Overwhelmed by their lives. Overwhelmed by their own to-do lists. Overwhelmingly overwhelmed.

Here's some truth I want to share with you: *overwhelm isn't having too much to do; it's not knowing where to start.*

But knowing where to begin can be incredibly difficult when we are too busy saying yes to every opportunity that knocks on our doors (even the ones we don't love), when we pile other people's priorities on our plates (and push aside our own), and when we worry about keeping up with everyone else.

Real productivity helps us know where to start. It's intentionally choosing to cut through the clutter and noise in our lives. It's discovering the happiness that comes when we center our lives on what is truly important to us and let go of the rest—it's the joy of missing out.

We have to begin finding the joy of missing out on that extra noise in our lives and instead find happiness in a life centered on what's truly important to us. We have to shift our mindset. I love the word *mindset*. It's one of my favorite words because your mindset has the power to change perspective, which means it has life-changing magic to it.

And while it's easy for me to tell you to change your mind, I know how difficult that can be. Maybe you are like me—an overachiever, a people pleaser, a perfecter—so you believe success has been defined by what you do, not who you are. You fill your days in pursuit of this illusion of success, just as I did, but deep down you feel there must be a better way. And you are so right.

Changing your mindset takes some work, but the beauty is when you begin to understand there's a huge difference between being busy and being productive. This is something so many of us struggle with because we falsely believe that we need to be busy, that we are *supposed* to fill our days.

Emily, in my Facebook group, shared: "For me [busy] feels like being the marble in the pinball machine versus following a road map from point A to point B. There's purpose to the latter, instead of just rolling around willy-nilly."

Willy-nilly. What a great word to describe what life feels like when we are always busy, when we're running like a hamster on a wheel, trying to keep up but not really going anywhere. We end our days frustrated and tired from working through lunch, multitasking while driving, and squeezing in emails between bedtime stories with our kids.

When we try to do too much, we overfill our plates with a multitude of tiny tasks and chores. We check a hundred things off our to-do lists, but when we slip into bed at night and our heads hit the pillow, we think, *Why didn't I get more done?*

We feel unsatisfied, unsuccessful, and unhappy even though we were busy all day long.

CHASING BUSY

We have to stop the glorification of busy. We need to change our mindset and redefine what it means to be productive. Productivity is not about doing more, it's doing what's most important. We need to stop trying to get more done and instead reset our focus on our own priorities. When we do that, our ideal lives can become our real, everyday lives.

Here's the catch: there's no magic system we can simply "plug into." Maybe you've tried productivity systems in the past and they didn't work. I understand. I felt exactly the same way back on that spring day when I spun in circles in my kitchen. My bookshelves were lined with the books of well-intentioned experts telling me that I needed to work smarter, not harder; that I needed the latest life hack; that I needed to find balance. But their rigid systems didn't work for me.

That's why productivity may have failed you in the past—it's the struggle to make your life fit the system when, in fact, it should be the system that fits *your* life. You can customize your productivity so that your life and your priorities are at the center.

Together we will custom design a system that works for you and your *life.* I want to show you that it's possible to be successful and still focus on your priorities. We don't have to sacrifice one for the other. It took that hard season in my life to open my eyes and see how *we hide behind our busy days and our long lists. We peek out and see that a richer life is available, but we don't feel entitled to it.* I'm here to tell you that you deserve that fulfilling life. We can lead extraordinary lives without the pressure of doing more, and we can live better by doing less.

For me, it began with letting go of the fear and worry that I wasn't doing enough—that I wasn't enough. I no longer spend my days being busy, and I no longer spin in circles feeling frustrated or worn thin.

I had to dedicate time to make this shift. I made it a priority to spend more intentional time with the important people in my life and to reinvent my time blocks to make sure they always sit at the front and center of my day. I dedicated myself to creating a productivity system that allowed bigger pockets of focused time for work and for home. And I am much happier for it.

We will build this unique blueprint together using the four steps of the liveWELL Method—the process I created that has allowed me to reclaim my time and enabled me to live the life I love. This same method has already helped women everywhere, just like you, live happy, productive lives. Women* who once felt overwhelmed but now use phrases like:

"I found myself—the self I was before I had kids . . . the one who
     dreamed about the future."
"I actually finish tasks before deadlines and have seen my self-
     confidence increase."
"I no longer feel like a failure if I don't do everything."
"In my heart of hearts, I believe I am making really good choices for
     myself, my health, and my family."

You'll meet some of these women on the pages that follow. They are from all walks of life—empty nesters, young moms, single professionals—and you'll see how they've transformed their lives. You'll read about their struggles, their lightbulb moments, and their successes.

The liveWELL Method is a series of small, huge movements: easy to manage and simple to implement, yet monumental in the impact they make on your daily life. In its most basic form, the liveWELL Method will help you design a life centered around your priorities. The four-step process will help you customize systems and strategies and design them to work *for you*. Let me unpack each of these steps for you now:

---

* Thank you to Julie, Melanie, Anna, and Michele for allowing me to share your wins here.

DISCOVERY: Because *you* are at the center—not the system—we begin by working together to discover your unique purpose and identify the priorities in your life. We will create a North Star to serve as your personal guide to help you make choices and begin to focus on what's important.

CLARITY: Using what we discovered in step one, we will learn how to choose the projects and tasks that will have the most impact on your goals and priorities. We will create effective boundaries and learn an easy framework to help clarify what is important and what is not.

SIMPLICITY: Even while living a priority-centered life, you still have all those not-so-glamorous tasks to accomplish—from home chores to finances. We will work together to simplify these systems and design personalized processes to help both your work and home life run with less effort.

HARMONY: Now that we have discovered your purpose, clarified what's important to you, and built a solid foundation of simplified systems to help things run smoothly, we will work to pull it all together and create harmony so you can begin living a life you love.

Each step in the process is designed to build on the preceding steps, helping you design a productive life. When you are productive, you place your priorities at the front and center of each and every day. And when your priorities are the focus, you can finally enjoy the whitespace—you can allow yourself to slow down and embrace the calm.

If this seems daunting, let me be honest with you: What's written in these chapters isn't rocket science. None of it is complex, difficult to follow, or hard to understand. It's amazingly simple. You know why? It's really about the choices we make and the mindsets we create for ourselves. The hardest part is making the decision to start.

THE JOY OF MISSING OUT

You know that life you've been dreaming about? The one you visit in your head when you have a spare moment to breathe . . . maybe in the shower or waiting in line for your morning coffee?

What's *missing* in that daydream? The feeling of being stretched too thin? I bet that's missing. Or the hectic pace? Gone. What about the heavy weight of obligations you've said yes to out of guilt? Not there.

There's joy in these missing pieces. There's happiness nestled right there, waiting to be had. Let's go get that—let's work together to make your ideal life a reality.

 ## LET ME HELP

I'll be with you every step of the way. In fact, to help you even more, I've created a companion email series you can access while reading this book. Think of it as a way to have me right alongside you, encouraging you and supporting you throughout this journey. I'll share extra resources and offer free downloads with activities that allow you to dive deeper into the process.

You can sign up for the free email series here: joyofmissingout.com/email. I'll see you in your inbox.

Tonya

PURSUE
DISCOVERY

Discover your priorities and purpose so that you can stop trying to do "all the things."

You may feel like you are wandering, a little lost in uncertainty. You crave more in life, but you don't know how to make your ideal day a reality, how to turn it into your everyday life. This is the perfect place to begin.

Discovery is the first step in the liveWELL Method because productivity should be customized to you and the life you want to live. Each of us is unique in where we want to shine our light, so we need to begin by solving the question of who we really are.

In this section, we will dig a little deeper into you and your unique priorities. We will uncover some of the false beliefs that may be holding you back and keeping you from the exceptional life you deserve. We'll work side by side to discover who you really are. Everything we build together in designing this productive life will be based on this foundation—it's centered on you.

CHAPTER 1

DISCOVER YOURSELF

Create the highest, grandest vision possible for your life, because you become what you believe.
OPRAH WINFREY

"What did you do today?"

The question was posed innocently enough, in between bites of dinner. I was leaning across the table, cutting Jack's chicken into tiny pieces, and I felt the knife skitter across the plate like a record skipping.

I knew John was genuinely interested in how I'd spent my day. But every evening when he asked me that question, I would feel the sweat begin to form on my hands and sense my heartbeat quickening ever so slightly.

I hated that question.

I hated it because it made me feel small. It made me feel like I needed to justify how I'd spent the last twelve hours of my day—not to him, but to myself. I thought I needed to prove I had spent my day being the best worker, the best mom, the best friend, the best volunteer, the best . . . well, everything.

And yet I always fell a little short. Not quite there. I believed I hadn't worked hard enough or long enough, I hadn't crossed off enough items on my ever-growing task list, or I hadn't been patient enough and fussed at the kids too much.

It didn't matter that I had run myself ragged all day long. It didn't matter that I filled every single moment, cramming 36 hours' worth of tasks into a 24-hour day. Quite honestly, most nights when the question was posed, my mind went absolutely blank like a chalkboard wiped clean. What *had* I done all day? When I frantically scoured the edges of my brain, I over-looked the multitude of jobs I had fulfilled throughout my day: mother, business owner, friend, teacher. The list went on and on.

If I had paused and taken a deep breath, I would have remembered I had answered a solid handful of customer emails, taken the kids to the library, chased them around the playground, used the in-between moments to toss in several loads of laundry, and made some serious progress on my new website. I would have given myself the grace to see what everyone else around me saw: *a woman who was doing her very best.*

But I couldn't see it. Instead of sharing all my wins, I rattled off what I *hadn't* done. I forgot to sign up Jack for art class; I didn't get a chance to stop at the post office; I wasn't able to finish with the blog post; and—

"Wow," John cut in jokingly, "didn't you do anything right today?"

In my mind, I hadn't. Hot tears streamed down my face because I could not see a single thing I'd done "right." Always falling a little short. I was good about seeing the good in others, but I never could seem to count my own marbles.

MARBLE JAR MOMENTS

Are you familiar with the marble jar trick? It's an old tactic teachers have used forever. I used it myself in my years when I stood at the front of a classroom. It's simple, really—every time the kids do something good, you drop a marble in a jar. When the jar fills up, well, that's when the class gets a reward.

But it's not just the reward that's exciting. That fresh marble makes a solid, satisfying clink as it bounces around in the jar. The kids' eyes get big and round when you hold up the marble, and they quiet down just to hear it rattle its way into the jar.

For the years I taught, I was a big believer in the power of the marble jar, and with great reason—it reinforces good work. We all want to be recognized for our efforts, don't we? We want credit for all the good we've done, which is why I believe we all have an invisible marble jar we carry around with us, begging to be filled.

Got up and worked out . . . marble in the jar! Made the kids' lunch . . . marble in the jar—wait, it was a *healthy* lunch . . . *two* marbles in the jar! And so our day continues with marbles clinking and filling up our jars.

The problem with these imaginary jars comes when something doesn't go quite right. We forget an important ingredient for dinner or we miss a deadline at work, and we don't just say, "Oops! No marble in the jar." We feel so defeated that we loosen our grip and allow our jar to slip out of our hands and crash onto the floor.

Marbles and broken glass are everywhere. It doesn't matter that the jar was almost full. It doesn't matter that we had done really well. All. Day. Long.

Instead of picking up those perfectly good marbles we earned, we decide we need to hustle to earn more marbles. We overfill our schedules with tasks and errands, desperately trying to refill our jars, which seem to shatter again and again throughout our day.

Our days are filled with far too many of these marble jar moments, aren't they? These moments when our marbles are scattered everywhere so we can no longer count them. We have to make it stop.

But too many of us tie our self-worth to our busyness. Stress and over-whelm are badges of honor declaring our worthiness. *We falsely believe that if we are* not *busy, we are failing.* In the pursuit of finding balance, we try to do everything, but the more we do, the less we succeed.

IT'S LIKE RIDING A BIKE

This idea of doing it all—and doing it well—is the problem I have with the concept of balance. Balance sounds nice, but it's nothing more than a productivity buzzword, an empty promise that leads us to falsely believe we should be able to do everything equally.

If life is perfectly balanced, we aren't really moving forward; instead, we are spinning chaotically like a top. We can take charge of our destinies only when we let go of balance and decide the direction we want our lives to go. Movement, in any direction, requires shifting—it requires counterbalance.

Think about balance like riding a bike. A bike has the ability to move in a deliberate direction. It requires some equilibrium to stay upright, but have you ever tried to balance on a bike that's perfectly still? It's almost impossible. We have to lean forward a bit and start gathering momentum by pushing on the pedals. The energy we create keeps us from falling over.

With a bike, we can choose to turn and move along a path we really want. We can go left or right by shifting our balance—we have to move away from perfect balance in order to turn. If we continue to lean heavily to the side, though, we will topple over. We need to counterbalance, readjusting our center of gravity to keep the bike upright and moving forward on this new path.

You see, *magic doesn't happen when life is centered and balanced—it happens when we lean into our priorities.* When we start concentrating on what is truly important to us, we *will* go out of balance.

Let's explore this idea together and apply it to real life. While we are all different, our lives are made up of the same three buckets that need to be filled: work, home, and personal.

> **WORK:** This area is what we consider our job. This might be running your own business or working in a small office or for a Fortune 500 company. Our work doesn't need to be tied to an income—it

might be that your job is CEO of the Home because you are a stay-at-home parent or a student going to school.

PERSONAL: This section of our lives is tied to relationships and inter-actions. This includes the connections we have with people like our significant others, our families, our friends, and the world around us. Our life goals, hobbies, and health all fall into this bucket because they are part of our relationship with ourselves.

HOME: This area includes the tasks and projects that keep life run-ning smoothly. While our personal bucket is about emotional needs, home is where our basic needs are met. This bucket includes chores and tasks like cleaning the house, running kids to activi-ties, and keeping up with daily happenings. Home is an important bucket because it helps us feel safe and secure.

Each of these areas is important, but balance implies that all three must be perfectly equal. We believe we need to distribute our time, energy, and focus in each of these areas evenly. Here's some truth I want to share with you—there's no way to keep all these buckets evenly filled, to keep them balanced all the time. It's simply not possible.

Creating an extraordinary life for ourselves requires moving away from balance, because when we lean into a priority—when we give time to the most important things—we have to take that time away from something else. We cannot give equal time to all the tasks on our lists.

Let me explain. We all have three key resources available to share with the world—*time, energy,* and *focus.* Each of these elements, though, is a depleting commodity; once it's invested, it's gone forever. You cannot get it back. By far, these are the most valuable resources we have to give. But in an effort to make our buckets feel like they are somewhat even, we spread these resources out far and wide, making little to no impact. We end up stretching ourselves thin, exhausting ourselves.

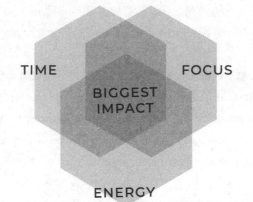

When we combine these three elements, though, we'll see the exact opposite—we'll discover exceptional results. This is true in all the areas of our lives, including our relationships, our work, and, yes, our productivity. We need all three to work united together to make the biggest impact possible in our days. We will dive deeper into each of these elements in section 2, but it's important to understand the power these three hold.

When we get caught up in the idea of balance, we are busy trying to make everything even. We don't concentrate our time, energy, and focus to move in the direction we *really* want to go. In chasing this illusion of balance, we end up creating a life that feels busy—not meaningful. We have to be willing to go out of balance. We need to be willing *not* to do everything. That's the real magic.

WHAT DO YOU BELIEVE?

Balance is just one of the stories we tell ourselves. We all have a library of folklore filled with stories about ourselves that we believe: we are supposed to be a certain way, have a certain job, or live a certain life. But the question we need to ask ourselves is: *Are these stories even true?*

Over time we all accumulate beliefs about ourselves and about life. These stories we tell ourselves again and again gain a mythology-like quality and begin to feel like truth. Often these stories are steeped in other people's truths—in their ideas and opinions that we've gathered together and made our own.

We hold ourselves up to the high standards these stories demand, even when they aren't realistic. These stories are almost always written in absolutes, using the words *always* and *never*:

A good mom never hires a babysitter to give herself some alone time.
A good friend always returns a text within ten minutes.
A good boss never leaves work before anyone else on the team.

Are these statements true? Are they fair? We set ourselves up for unrealistic expectations no one could achieve, and, in fact, we wouldn't hold *anyone else* to these standards. These stories seem innocent enough. After all, they are just stories, right? But don't be fooled—these stories transform into limiting beliefs that hold us back; they demand that we spend our time in ways that don't *really* fit into the life we want. We follow their strict rules because we think we should. We think we are supposed to behave a certain way, and so we do.

One of the stories I told myself for years was that good moms stayed home. They had cookies baked when their kids got off the bus, and they volunteered almost daily at their kids' school. That's what my mom did, so I set those requirements for myself.

But those rules didn't work for me, which made me feel guilty because I believed I *should have been* fulfilled by those things—but I wasn't. I *really* like working, and my work schedule made it hard to fulfill these strict requirements I had set for myself. I couldn't let go of the guilt that was telling me I wasn't a good mom. It ate away at me and my happiness. I had to change my thinking; I had to shift my definition of a good mom and what it means to me.

I don't stay at home, but I make a conscious effort to be there in the afternoons to help with homework. I'm not a lead volunteer like my mom was—I'm a supporting volunteer.

I quieted the stories in my head and reset my expectations to make them realistic for my life. I'm not going to say I've completely gotten rid of the guilt, but I feel so much better because I changed my way of thinking. I do what I can, and my story now tells me: *a good mom loves her children the best she can.*

DECONSTRUCTING OUR STORIES

What do you think defines a good person? Is it that a good person always puts others first even if it means they don't get to work on their goals? That a good person never accepts help? Or a good person doesn't make time for themselves?

I want you to fill in this blank for me. Don't overthink it. What is the first thing that comes to mind: A good person always _is kind to others_

And then ask yourself: Is this statement *really* true? Or am I just holding myself up to a high standard I can never actually achieve? We need to recognize the limiting beliefs that are holding us back.

Why do we have these limiting beliefs, and where did they start? There is a point in our lives where we seem to go from confident to questioning—from being assertive and sure to hesitant and uncertain. For many of us, there's a tiny little blip on our life maps, somewhere between elementary school and high school, where we lost our self-assurance in who we are.

Ask any kindergartner what they are good at, and you'll need to sit through a laundry list of topics: art, running, painting, climbing trees, eating potato chips—seriously, five-year-olds think they are amazing at everything! But wait ten years and ask the very same child, and she'll think of almost nothing; at best you'll maybe hear one or two things she believes she excels in. What happens to us in this space of time? How do we lose our belief in ourselves? We've allowed the world to define us and reinforce these limiting beliefs, but it's time to break through.

YOUR UNKNOWN STRENGTH

We've all heard tales of people who suddenly acquire superhuman strength to lift a car when a child is trapped beneath or who heave huge slabs of concrete rubble aside after an earthquake. While not all of us may experience a surge in adrenaline like that, we all have a superhuman ability inside us to transform. Sometimes it's just a limiting belief, the idea that you simply cannot do something, that restricts you.

———

In early October 2009, eighty-seven-year-old Warren climbed on the roof of his home to make a quick repair. One week later, he was diagnosed with a cancer so severe that by Thanksgiving his family was carrying out the mournful task of planning his funeral. His widow, Gwen, was suddenly on her own.

Gwen had never lived alone—at the age of eighteen, she had moved from her parents' house directly into her new husband's home once he returned from war. She had never paid an electric bill or used a credit card; in her eight decades she had never once pumped her own gas. With Warren's death, her family fretted about how Gwen would hold up. They worried about how she would survive when she'd never really done anything on her own, but Gwen surprised them all.

When talk came up after the funeral about her moving, she put her foot down and insisted she would live alone in the home she had built with Warren. And she did. She made adjustments and created a whole new independent life for herself.

Gwen didn't just survive—she thrived. Why? Because, at the age of eighty-three, she was willing to understand she had other roles to live. She wasn't just a widow—she was a mother, a grandmother, a pie baker, a friend. She took on a new role as encourager for the elderly. She had a regular rotation of visits to women in the nursing homes—a group she lovingly referred to as "my old ladies." And now Gwen is gunning for one hundred because, in her own words, she has a lot to live for. I know this because Gwen happens to be my grandma.

To tell you that we were shocked when she proclaimed that she would be just fine on her own would be an understatement, but she had a strength inside her no one knew about. In fact, *she* didn't even know this strength existed. She didn't allow herself to be defined by her eighty-three years of being dependent on someone else. Sometimes we have to let go of our old stories.

CHANGE YOUR CONJUNCTION

I've met thousands of people through speaking and workshops, and many have shared with me that they identify closely with one role. Often, if it's women of a certain age, it's the role of mother, but it might be "career woman" or "caregiver." They look at this role and feel that it defines every part of who they are, which leaves almost no room for anything else—certainly no room for other priorities or dreams that fall outside these tight parameters. I hear stories like these:

> *I can be a mom* OR *I can chase my dream of opening my business.*
> *I can be a career woman* OR *a hands-on parent.*
> *I can take care of my elderly parents* OR *pursue my art career.*

They fool themselves with their stories and conclude that life is an either/or situation.

Donna,* a woman in my liveWELL Method course, shared with me that she wasn't sure about the direction of her life. In her own words, she felt "pretty much stuck." She had homeschooled her now-grown children for over a decade, followed by nursing and caring for her father until his

---

* Name has been changed.

Sometimes

WE HAVE TO LET GO

OF OUR

OLD STORIES

passing, and then, not long after that, she had taken charge of handling a relative's estate to alleviate the stress for her family. She had spent years in the role of caregiver—giving willingly and lovingly. But now she was in a space where she didn't have someone else defining her role, which felt scary.

When we spend a long time centered on one role, we often find it hard to look around and see other possibilities. Donna and I went through her answers to an exercise she had done as part of the course. She shared with me that she was an avid reader who enjoyed attending writers' conferences, craved time to read, and wished she had more time to spend on self-education. I told her, "You obviously have a love of books, authors, and writing . . . so I'm wondering, why isn't writing at the heart of your purpose?" I noticed, too, when she shared her ideal day, that she considered focused, uninterrupted writing time the highlight. But Donna struggled with this and admitted it was hard to switch gears.

The issue here was with the way Donna viewed herself. She limited herself to the role of caretaker and left no room for anything else. She didn't feel right letting the focus be on herself after spending a lifetime focusing on others.

Donna needed to add an *and* in her "job description."

Instead of only filling the role of caregiver, why not open it up? Why couldn't she be someone who cares for her family *and* spends time pursuing a passion for writing?

We all need to add some *and* to our lives. But let me be clear: this is not about piling more on our plates—it's not about adding more to our day. It's about opening our eyes and shifting the way we look at who we are and reclaiming our lives by placing what's important to us front and center.

Because so many of us live in a state of either/or, we tend to push aside other things we really want to do. Far too many of us have pushed aside our aspirations because we believe we don't have time or don't have the right to pursue them. This is just another story we need to reset.

One of the ways to stop these unhealthy stories is to take inventory of what we believe. To do this, ask yourself, *Do I believe my life is ready for growth, or is my path fixed?*

If you believe your life is ready for growth, then you see yourself as fluid, a work in progress. Your fate is one of betterment and opportunities to explore and discover. If you believe your life is fixed, however, you view yourself as unchangeable. Basically, you believe you are who you are and your destiny is already set. Your objective might be to go through life avoiding failure, which also means you avoid challenge.

Which one are you? Are you ready to effect some change in your life even with the possibility of experiencing discomfort? Or do you want to stick with the status quo and not deal with disruption? Because change is a disruption, it's something people tend to avoid—even if it means staying on the same old path heading in a direction they don't really love.

I'll be honest. I know that sticking with the status quo is easier. After all, it's a well-worn path—we know where it turns, where the rocks are . . . But do you like where it's heading? The road to change is full of uncertainty, so it can be scary. It might even feel uncomfortable. But we need some discomfort to make a change.

When we are doing something new, we are shifting our mindset, and that means something fulfilling is just around the corner. I'll be there, next to you, guiding you through it.

It will be worth it, I promise.

LET ME HELP

Want to dive a little deeper? I've got some extra resources to share with you. Make sure to sign up for the email companion series that goes along with the book at joyofmissingout.com/email.

CHAPTER 2

DISCOVER CHOICE

It is our choices . . . that show what we truly
are, far more than our abilities.
J. K. ROWLING

I want you to make a choice:

A. I will choose my own path and priorities.
B. I will let others choose my path and priorities.

If you chose B, you might want to stop and put the book down. You won't like the rest of this chapter—or this book—because I believe we all want and need to be in charge of our choices. This is hard, though, especially when so many people believe they don't have ownership over their day.

Too often we hand over the reins, allowing others to imprison us with their own agendas and urgent fires that need putting out. We think we don't have control over how our day runs, but we do. We've simply forgotten that we have the ability to choose to spend time on our own priorities.

We all know what a priority is—it's something that is important to us. But the struggle for most people is understanding what is a priority and what isn't. After all, how can we prioritize when *everything* feels important?

When we treat everything as equal, it means nothing is a priority. It all gets jumbled together, and we begin to lose sight of what really matters. We believe we should be able to exhaust all the opportunities available. Because we don't want to miss out on anything, we treat everything as if it's important—even when it's not. This leaves us feeling like a dog chasing its tail.

The word *priority* did not exist until the fifteenth century. It simply wasn't a word. And then when it did finally merge into conversations, it was always singular—never *priorities*. And it stayed that way for about five hundred years, until suddenly it became plural.

And so we began our cultural belief that we should be treating more things on our list as priorities—even priorities that don't really belong to us. As Greg McKeown, author of *Essentialism*, noted, "Illogically, we reasoned that by changing the word we could bend reality. Somehow we would now be able to have multiple 'first' things."

In reality no one needs #allthethings, just the things that are truly fulfilling *to them*. It's hard to let things go, especially when there's a little bit of safety or comfort involved. Focusing your time, getting rid of some of the noise, and lasering in on your priorities sometimes takes some discomfort. I know this myself firsthand.

We need to discover the priorities that are unique to us, but first we have to take hold of this truth: *we must be willing to* not *have it all*.

IS IT TOO LATE TO CHANGE?

October in Asheville, North Carolina, is gorgeous. The weather dips into the cool temperatures of fall, and the mountains start to light up in brilliant oranges and reds. It's one of my favorite times of the year—every year except 2013.

I had started my own business years earlier, and I had grown it to the point where John could leave the corporate world and work alongside me. We worked shoulder to shoulder, putting our all into the business, and I loved working together. And yet, even though I should have been happy, I wasn't. I felt a deep nagging sense of dissatisfaction.

I couldn't put my finger on what it was—there wasn't one singular moment when the clouds parted in a made-for-TV moment and I realized this wasn't the life for me. I just knew I felt weighted down and heavy with the burden of waking up to a job that didn't really tick the boxes of what was important to me. I was spending my days spinning my wheels, chasing after a life that made me feel exhausted and empty.

Most of my days ended with me feeling defeated and unfulfilled because I didn't love what I was putting forth into the world. And that unhappiness with my work was starting to bleed into the other buckets of my life, making me feel hollow.

My business, though, was the sole income for our family. It provided food for our kids, it paid our mortgage—it allowed us to live. I owed that business a lot, but I dreamed of finding a life where I could feel full again and satisfied with my work. I dreamed of a life where John and I could continue to work alongside one another, but that seemed like a fantasy.

How could I possibly turn my back on a thriving business that paid my family's bills to pursue something new? A feeling of powerlessness loomed over me like a dark cloud.

I felt stuck. It seemed obvious to me that I had no choice—there were no other options.

WE HAVE A CHOICE

You may have experienced this feeling yourself. In fact, while reading this book, you may have thought to yourself, *That sounds nice, but there's no way I can make that happen in my life*, or *I would love to spend time on my personal priorities, but there's just too much to do.*

Let me lay a little tough love on you right now. *You can choose or let others choose for you. The choice is really yours.* Not making a choice *is* a choice. But so many of us have forgotten that we have a choice—it's a case of learned helplessness.

Have you ever experienced that feeling of having no control over your day? As if your world is so rigid and made up of so many rules you don't really get to choose the life you live? That, my friend, is learned helplessness. That feeling I was experiencing? Of being stuck (and the fact that I wanted to give up and not even think about how empty I felt)? That was my own learned helplessness rearing its ugly head.

The problem lies in where we allow this learned helplessness to take over, because this passivity can lead us to overlook opportunities for relief. A good example of this type of behavior is when a student studies for a test and yet still performs poorly. When it's time to study for the next test, she may believe there's no point because "she won't do well anyway," so she doesn't bother.

She seems to forget that for the first test, she went out late the night before or was distracted by an argument with her best friend. She only remembers that she studied and didn't do well; therefore, studying didn't help. She feels stuck and doesn't see any other choice, so she simply stops trying.

It's not reality that makes us feel stuck; it's the lens we use to view the world. Maybe you are tired of trying because it feels like it just doesn't seem to matter. I've felt this way too. There are times when we all just want to crawl back in bed and throw the covers over our heads because we are so overwhelmed with the chaotic rush of our days.

We can lose sight of who we are deep inside and what is most important to us. We are so busy struggling and fighting to keep our heads above the proverbial water that we seem to forget we can choose to tread water for a moment. We can allow ourselves a deep breath and time to scan the horizon—we can choose to swim to calmer waters.

When we gift ourselves with the ability to step back and choose, something powerful begins to happen. We strengthen our internal locus of control. In other words, we remember we have the ability to influence our own destiny instead of allowing the current to push us wherever it wants.

People with a strong internal locus of control believe they have the freedom and ability to make their own choices and determine what happens to them. Because of that, they are significantly happier and more motivated. Psychologists have found that an "internal locus of control has been linked with academic success . . . higher self-motivation and social maturity . . . lower incidences of stress and depression . . . and longer life span." We want to strengthen our internal locus of control and begin to understand that we have choices.

BUT I REALLY DON'T HAVE ANY CONTROL

If you're still saying, "That isn't true for me; I don't have any choices in my day." I hear you. You have a strict boss, an overbearing family member, an overly regimented schedule, a special-needs child, or something similar. Right?

———

I met Rhonda when I was speaking at a workshop event a while back, and I instantly liked her. With a flourishing career and a great family, she is what many would consider a successful woman juggling it all. Anyone looking at her life from the outside would believe she has it all together.

I had just led the group through an exercise where we began uncovering the heart of our priorities, and I asked Rhonda what she had discovered about herself. She walked me through her discoveries, but what I noticed was how much her eyes lit up when she mentioned yoga. I asked her to tell me more about her workout.

Immediately her face became animated as she told me all about her favorite morning yoga class—this was clearly one of the highlights of her day. I love when I see passion like this in other people; it lights me up. I asked her if she had been to class that morning, and something funny happened—the brightness in her eyes dimmed. "Oh no," she said, "I haven't been in at least six months. I haven't gone regularly for years."

Years? For something she clearly felt so passionate about? I pushed her on this, and she explained that it just wasn't possible. There was absolutely no way she could make it happen. She was far too busy and had too many people who needed her—it was just unrealistic to imagine being able to take morning yoga classes at all in her week, let alone every morning. So I pushed again, and she told me that her family relied on her too much for the mornings to run smoothly without her. So I pushed again. (Notice a theme here?)

Could the kids lay out their clothes the night before? She laughed lightly when I asked this and said, "Oh, I don't pick out their clothes. They get themselves dressed." One hurdle down.

Could lunches be made the night before? "Yes," she said, "and actually they could do it themselves, now that I think about it. That would help them be more independent." *Why, yes it would.* (And if there's one thing I love, it's independence in kids and parents who cultivate it.) We talked about how to make this process easier with designated spots for "lunch-approved" items in the fridge and pantry. Already I could see Rhonda's expression was a bit more hopeful. Two hurdles down.

Now the big one—driving the kids to school. Rhonda sheepishly admitted her kids were both in high school, and since the older one had a license, there was no reason they couldn't drive themselves. Hurdle number three came crashing down, and in that instant, the possibilities became endless. Yes, she could still take care of her kids *and* she could go to yoga. Maybe every day wasn't doable, but three times a week would be amazing at this point in her life.

Remember those stories we tell ourselves? I believe Rhonda was telling herself that *a good mom is there every morning to get her kids out the door.* And that story rang true for her, even while her kids were growing older and eventually didn't need her to be quite so hands-on. Rhonda's role was evolving, and sometimes when that's happening to us, it can be really hard to see. We want to believe our kids need us, and sometimes in the busy rush of our everyday life, we forget they are capable of being more independent.

At first blush, this evolution might make us feel a little sad, but really it's cause to celebrate. It means we are doing our job of raising kids to be strong adults. When we take a minute to realize this, we can drop a fresh marble in the jar.

Now that Rhonda could see this clearly, we sat down and made a plan that allowed time for her family to adjust to the changes in routine and for her to adjust her mindset too. We decided that once a week was a good place to start, so the first four weeks she'd go to yoga once a week. Then she would step it up to twice a week for eight weeks, followed later by three times a week. Suddenly this ideal vision for her morning was achievable because there was a series of choices Rhonda hadn't seen before.

We all have these invisible choices, don't we?

SQUIRREL STRATEGY

But what if there had been a real obstacle to Rhonda's plan? For example, what if neither of her kids were drivers? What then? I would encourage her to use the Squirrel Strategy.

I first heard this term from blind adventurist Erik Weihenmayer, and I think it accurately describes how we can approach problem solving, especially problems that feel unsolvable—you know, like Erik climbing Mount Everest without the ability to see.

Have you ever watched a squirrel aiming to get something she wants? Perched in a tree, tail twitching, she sees a bird feeder and is drawn to it. The homeowners, though, are smart, and they've added all kinds of obstacles to make it "squirrel-proof." Does our squirrel take a look, decide she has no chance of getting to the seeds, and toss in the towel? Absolutely not. A squirrel will attack the problem from all angles, testing and pushing the boundaries of what she knows she can and cannot do, until she sits triumphantly atop that feeder with a belly full of birdseed.

We can learn a thing or two from squirrels. We need to think outside the confines of what we know and discover our choices. We can look at our situation from all angles and see what choices we actually do have.

With some brainstorming and thinking outside the box, you can discover other options in a situation like Rhonda's:

Can you arrange for carpool and share driving duties with other parents?
Can your partner take over school drop-offs on certain mornings?

Can your kids walk to school with friends?
Can you find a before-school option for childcare?

The choices are there; you just have to be creative in looking for them.

There are always ways to buck the system, even systems with incredibly limiting choices. Research proves that seniors who push back against the rules in their assisted living facilities to assert small acts of independence live happier, healthier lives. Prison inmates who find ways to create their own positive choices are more successful when reentering society. Finding choices isn't only possible, it's essential to thrive. You just have to start actively looking for them—that's a choice in and of itself.

My question for you is: *Are you choosing to spend your time being busy, or are you choosing to focus your day on what matters most?*

CAN I BUILD SOMETHING NEW?

During that dark October in 2013, I remember looking out my back window and watching the wind whip past while leaves settled on our worn-out deck. It looked just as tired as I felt, so I grabbed a sledgehammer to start tearing it down.

Projects involving building and power tools are one of the things in life I truly enjoy. I wanted to rebuild that deck, but even more so, I wanted to see if I still had any fire left inside me. I was scared I no longer had the ability to feel the satisfaction I craved. Twenty minutes later, John appeared by my side with a hammer in hand. As with all things, we were in this together.

There we were, silently swinging and sweating side by side, tearing away the old pieces of wood, and it felt *great*. Not good, not okay—I felt alive. We worked on that deck while the weather changed from cool to downright cold; I stepped back after a solid week of hard work and saw the structure we had created. I knew right then that we would be okay. There was still drive and passion inside me. I could still build something new.

In that moment, I had no idea what that "something new" would be, but I knew I couldn't keep slogging through my days feeling numb. I understood I needed to discover what was at the heart of what I wanted to do. I have to be honest and admit this uncertainty was scary, but the idea of continuing on the same path I was on was even scarier. I didn't want to waste any more time living an unfulfilled life.

ONE HUNDRED YEARS OF BEING YOU

We have a limited amount of time in our lives, so it's important to spend it on the things that matter most. It can be really hard to think about our priorities and time because both concepts are so abstract. I'll make it a little easier by making time seem a little more physical.

Here's what 100 years would look like if I were to give each year a concrete shape:

100 YEARS

Now, before you begin to feel like you have plenty of time, let's adjust the scenario a *tiny* bit. Most of us won't live 100 years. The current life span of an American male is approximately 77 years, and for an American female it's 81. For the sake of argument, let's make it easy and say that you'll live to be 80 years old. We'll adjust our diagram slightly by knocking 20 years off at the bottom:

100 YEARS

Look at that—already we've begun to realize that time is finite. It's a commodity that continues to disappear. Now, for the sake of this example, let's say that you are 35 years old:

100 YEARS

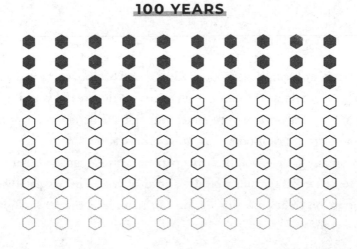

The black is the time that you've already used—there's obviously no getting it back—and the open spaces are the time you have left. How do you feel about your time now?

Let's look at the diagram again but in a slightly different way—in terms of months. You start your life with 960 months. Now, as a 35-year-old, you still have quite a few months ahead of you. Some people have more; some have less. But for the sake of argument, let's say since you're living to the age of 80, you've got 540 months of your life left—more than half:

80 YEARS

(IN MONTHS)

So when we are talking about an ideal vision of who we are and what we are doing, what does that mean? Let's focus on the area of your life where you spend the majority of your time: your job. Whether you work in an office or you're a stay-at-home parent, you have a job.

Like many people, you probably plan to retire at age 65, so at the age of 35, you have 30 years of working ahead of you. That's what I want to concentrate on right now: this section in the middle, the 30 years of work ahead of you:

80 YEARS

That translates into 360 months—7,800 workdays. Or to put it more succinctly, 1,560 Mondays to roll out of bed, put your feet on the floor, and make your way to work:

30 YEARS

7,800 WORKDAYS | **1,560** MONDAYS

So you have a choice. Do you want to spend those Mondays rolling out of bed and heading to a job that fulfills you and brings you closer to your ideal vision? Or do you stay where it's comfortable, where you are now?

Now, you may think, *I will shift someday. It will happen, just not today. Maybe I will start in a year:*

29 YEARS

7,540 WORKDAYS | **1,508** MONDAYS

Okay, you are down to 7,540 workdays. What about waiting 5 years:

25 YEARS

6,500 WORKDAYS | **1,300** MONDAYS

Now you only have 1,300 Mondays to work in a job that fulfills you. Maybe you wait 10 years, so you have 20 left:

20 YEARS

5,200 WORKDAYS | **1,040** MONDAYS

My point is, time doesn't stop. It's finite, and we have to treat it as such when it comes to our priorities and our vision of where we want to be. You have more time left in your life right now in this very minute than you will have an hour from now. There is not another point in your lifetime when you'll have the luxury of the amount of time you have right this very second.

This is why you need to keep those priorities in focus and why you can feel the joy of missing out on the rest. If there's something you *really* want to do, today is the day to start. It's possible for your future to look brighter, for you to focus on the things that are important to you. But to do that, your priorities have to take priority. It's possible to have a job that makes you happy and to spend time on the things you really want.

Here is an example of how I've used this concrete diagram to help me focus on my priorities, specifically those not related to my career. For me a top priority is my kids. I want to show you how I was able to shift my mindset so that my time with them was more of a priority, and how I was able to let go of the rest.

When my kids were born, they had 100 years laid out before them like a blank slate:

100 YEARS

And, yes, I think they will live to 100, because by the time they are old and gray, science will have advanced so much they'll probably be able to transfer their heads over to robot bodies or something crazy like that.

I am lucky enough to get to live with these kids for the first 18 years. And if you look at it on the time map, you'll see, in the grand scheme of things, that's not very much. It's less than 20 percent of their lives:

18 YEARS

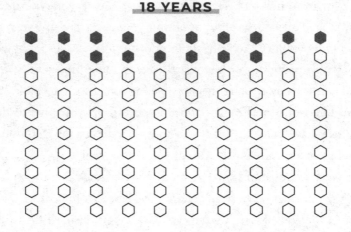

As much as I love them, I'm not planning on having them move back home after they become adults. I only have 18 years to soak up that time, to try and impart some values, and to give them a foundation to become independent adults.

When I think about the time I have with them, I think of it in terms of Friday nights. Why Friday nights? Well, for me, Friday night is the best night of the week. The weekend is laid out before me wide open, and Friday nights are for pizza and movies or games or some other time spent together. Friday nights are important to me. I started out with 936 of these Friday nights:

936 FRIDAY NIGHTS

By the time my kids are ten years old, my number of Friday nights has gone down:

416 FRIDAY NIGHTS

Only 416, less than half, are left, and at this point they aren't able to spend every Friday night with me because they have other things going on, like sleepovers, movies with friends, and so on.

And then, they get to high school:

208 FRIDAY NIGHTS

There are precious few Friday nights left, around 208. Suddenly these Friday nights that seemed so plentiful are now dwindling down to almost zero. They've become even more valuable to me. They are a depleting commodity, and they are depleting at a much faster rate than I'd like to believe.

So we begin hoarding our Friday nights and treating them a little bit better. But shouldn't we be doing that all along? *Shouldn't we be treating our priorities like priorities all the time?* That's what we need to keep in mind.

My kids have 100 years of Friday nights on the day they are born. But I only have 18 years' worth of those Friday nights with them. I want to treat Friday nights as a priority in this season of life I'm in right now.

When I look at this limited time I have, it reminds me that we all have seasons we live through. Seasons when our lives are hard and seasons where life comes easy, but in the scheme of 100 years, those seasons are a mere fraction of the time we have. Later in life, when my kids are grown, Friday night might not hold the power it does now. And that's a good perspective to remember. *Seasons pass, life ebbs and flows, but our priorities are what anchor us.*

The point I want you to focus on is that we are all lucky enough to be on this earth for a finite amount of time—it's up to us to maximize that time and live our lives to the fullest. Living a life with our priorities guiding us is the key to a happy life—a life that feels well lived.

FINDING MY NORTH STAR

After rebuilding my deck, I had gained the knowledge that I could build something new, but it wasn't enough to move me forward. I needed direction. I remember sitting hunched over on the edge of my bed, palms faceup on my knees, and begging God not for answers but for guidance. I asked him to help illuminate my way so I could see the path he had designed for me. I gave myself a week to dive into the process, and in those seven days I dug deep. I knew taking the time to discover my purpose, my North Star, would provide the guidance I needed.

The process I created for myself, which I'll be sharing with you in the next chapter, helped me realize I wanted to do something with productivity, because this was what had allowed me to create harmony in my own life. I found that even though I hadn't stood in front of a classroom for many years, my teacher heart was still a big part of me because I love educating others. I also realized how much joy it brought me to coach women and to see them feel confident and happy. I had found my North Star. I had found my fire.

Taking the time to be still, to listen to my inner voice, and to let my North Star guide me made all the difference. I decided to create inkWELL Press Productivity Co., a company focused on productivity and planning. We design, produce, and sell products that help people center their lives on what's important to them. To fulfill my vision, I knew there also had to be a part of the business that focused on education, teaching others how to identify their priorities and create their own productivity systems. I decided everything we did had to be filtered through my North Star. In other words, I would create a laser-focused business centered around my vision.

Don't get me wrong, it wasn't easy. I made plenty of mistakes. Just because you are on your path doesn't mean it's free of stones or brambles to fight through. But even when I felt like I didn't know what I was doing, I was confident because I was following my North Star. And that's where I am today. Still growing, still moving forward (and still making some mistakes), but most importantly living a life I love with my priorities guiding every step.

YOUR TOP REGRETS

I don't want to live a life of regret, and you don't either. You deserve more.

Bronnie Ware was a woman who wasn't sure what she wanted to do in life, but she knew she wanted to help others. She found a job working as a palliative care nurse, a job that really suited her. She was a great caretaker and even better listener, both of which are key traits when caring for the seriously ill.

She listened to her patients' stories and memories, and within the first year she began to notice a pattern emerging. Regret. Regret for a lifetime of choices. Oftentimes these decisions were ones her patients didn't even realize they had made. Over the course of her eight-year career, she saw this theme of regret appear again and again with different patients, from different backgrounds, with very different lives:

> *I wish I'd had the courage to live life true to myself, not the life others expected of me.*
> *I wish I hadn't worked so hard.*
> *I wish I'd had the courage to express my feelings.*
> *I wish I'd stayed in touch with my friends.*
> *I wish I'd let myself be happier.*

That last one gets me the most—*I wish I'd let myself be happier.* I think the thing that stands out to me is the phrase "let myself." Why *don't* we allow ourselves to be happy, to become the people we want to be?

"Isn't it selfish to think of your own priorities?" I've had some people ask. And, to be honest, this question makes me laugh. You know why? When you become the person you want to be, this not only enhances your own life but benefits the lives of everyone around you.

Think about it. When I broke down the concept of time, what did you immediately start thinking about as you began to see your weeks dwindling down? What important ideas or people popped into your mind? I'll let you in on a little secret: *those are your priorities.*

So, I'll ask you, is it selfish to think of them?

If I'm guessing, I'd say family and friends were at the top of your list. Maybe you thought of something tied to creating a better life or perhaps a dream or goal that you haven't pursued. Those things you thought of, were they just for you? Or were they about cultivating relationships, providing security for those you care about, and maybe even creating an impact in the world around you? That's not selfish. That's life-giving.

It's not selfish to live a fulfilling, happy life, but we often wrestle with feeling guilty about enjoying our time or loving what we're doing, especially when we see others struggling. But here's the catch: unhappiness serves no one.

Happiness is not a limited resource. You are not going to use it all up. If anything, it's a resource that exponentially grows when it's cultivated. Happiness spreads.

Your happiness isn't defined by others, it is defined by you and the daily choices you make. Living a life centered on your priorities is making a choice to be happy, and it's okay to choose happy.

Allowing your priorities to sit front and center is a daily decision. It's purposely choosing to let go of what is unimportant—or at least loosening your grasp. Discovering your North Star, just as I did, will help with making these choices easier, and that's what I want us to dive into next.

HAPPINESS

ISN'T DEFINED BY OTHERS

IT IS **DEFINED BY** *You*
AND THE DAILY CHOICES YOU MAKE

CHAPTER 3

DISCOVER YOUR NORTH STAR

I am not afraid of storms, for I am learning how to sail my ship.

LOUISA MAY ALCOTT

Imagine this: You are sitting at your kitchen table on a beautiful spring morning. You leisurely munch on your toast, strawberry jelly dripping onto your plate, while you scroll your phone for the morning's news. Suddenly your eyes widen as you spy your own name on the screen—an announcement of your death.

How would this make you feel? What would the article say about your legacy? How would you be remembered?

While this may seem far-fetched, this little fiction is based on the true story of Alfred Nobel, a scientist credited with around 355 inventions. His most notable was a stable explosive to replace the highly volatile (and very dangerous) nitroglycerin. Alfred named his invention "dynamite."

Alfred felt secure about his legacy, but that changed in 1888 when his brother Ludvig died while in France. Instead of publishing Ludvig's obituary, however, the newspaper mistakenly wrote: "Dr. Alfred Nobel, who became rich by finding ways to kill more people faster than ever before, died yesterday." The article was titled "The Merchant of Death Is Dead."

Yikes. There's a headline that would make you spit out your toast.

Alfred had believed dynamite was a gift to humanity, as it made working conditions safer for thousands. To see printed in black and white that this was not how he was perceived devastated him. Provoked by this event and disappointed by how he would be remembered, Nobel set out to change his legacy. He set aside a bulk of his estate to establish prizes to honor men and women for outstanding achievements in physics, chemistry, medicine, literature, and in working toward peace.

Alfred clarified his North Star, and the Nobel Prize became an extension of his clearer focus. When he did die in 1896, he was remembered as a humanitarian and an advocate for the sciences, certainly not as a merchant of death. He had made a conscious choice to redirect his life and to create his own legacy.

WHY DO WE NEED A NORTH STAR?

The North Star has long been known as a constant in the night sky. Throughout history, it has guided sailors and adventurers on the path to their ultimate destinations, keeping them from being lost long before there were maps. The North Star is the beacon shining through the dark unknown, lighting our path.

While we may not be sailors, we still need a constant in our life to help guide us through the darkness. Here's the hard fact: *we don't just find ourselves on a fulfilling, deeply satisfying path—we create it for ourselves.* The clarity comes from within us.

Our purpose and our priorities need to drive our productivity. The more we allow our North Star to guide us, the more productive and fulfilled we will become. *When we live our life using our North Star, we take ownership of our legacy.*

When we don't define our North Star, we allow others to define it for us.* And often this means we are spending time being busy instead of focusing on moving forward in the direction we truly want to go. Our North Star determines how we want to spend our time and, most importantly, guides our decisions.

I want you to think about this: How many times a week, or even a day, do you make decisions? Even those small decisions you aren't actively thinking about, like scrolling through your phone instead of engaging in conversation with your loved ones. We forget we are actively making those choices. Having a North Star guides you in your daily life and drives the direction of your choices—big and small.

Decisions become easier when we have this foundation of confidence. At its core, *productivity is about making a series of choices.* Choices have the power to make us genuinely productive rather than simply busy. By not making choices and allowing others' priorities to become our own, we will never feel truly productive, no matter how many tasks we check off our lists.

We have to sort through the opportunities and activities and choose to focus on what's most important. I realize that finding the joy of missing out—in saying no—isn't easy; it's a hard choice to make at times. That's true for all of us, myself included. Don't worry, though. We are going to work through this idea together. (And trust me, when we get to section 4, it will be so much easier for you to say no.)

DOING, DREAMING, AND DEFINING

In chapter 2 I shared my story about needing to discover my North Star. I remember going online and searching for answers. I knew my current path wasn't the right one for me, but what *was* the right path? Why couldn't someone just tell me? Every article I found began with the phrase "Start by

---

* If you're reading this, you already chose at the start of the last chapter to not let this happen.

CHOICES

HAVE THE **POWER** TO MAKE US

genuinely

PRODUCTIVE

RATHER THAN SIMPLY BUSY

writing down your purpose." I thought I would tear my hair out! I wanted to scream at the computer because that was the problem—I had no idea.

I knew there was a path that was destined for me, but it had become so overrun with weeds I could no longer see it. I felt lost. At times I would literally imagine myself alone in an overgrown woods, turning in circles with no idea of where to step next. I was scared. I was scared to move and scared to stand still.

I didn't really know what my North Star was—I had to discover it for myself. And I think that's one of the most important parts of the process: ownership. You have to take this journey; you have to do the work because this is *your* path. The good, the bad, and the ugly: *It belongs to you. So own it.*

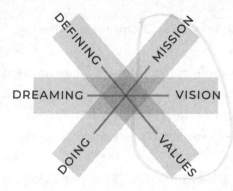

Our North Star is a combination of our mission, vision statement, and core values. Each one answers the question of who you are at your heart. The mission statement tells us what we are doing now, the vision statement tells of where we want to be, and the core values tell us how these can be defined through our actions. Like pieces of a puzzle, they come together to create the completed picture of why we make the choices we do. They become the North Star we need to guide us and help us navigate through decisions.

I cannot design this North Star for you; neither can your best friend or your family. Your North Star is uniquely yours. It's your own filter for guiding your behavior and choices—providing clear direction and guiding you to make the best decisions to help you achieve your goals. It's important to take the time to custom design it for yourself.

Some people find terms like *mission statement* and *core values* intimidating. It's almost like the words themselves are heavy because they feel so important. I think many people believe these words work to define them—now, always, and forever. This idea is what causes a huge stumbling block—no wonder it feels so heavy! Yes, they do add value and structure to our lives, but the process doesn't have to feel intimidating or frightening.

In Harvard psychologist Daniel Gilbert's TED Talk "The Psychology of the Future Self," he said, "Human beings are works in progress that mistakenly think they are finished. The person you are right now is transient, as fleeting and as temporary as all the people you've ever been. The one constant in our lives is change."

We are constantly evolving, learning, and growing. We are in a constant state of change, so why would we assume our values and priorities are fixed? Take a minute and think of who you were just two years ago. What were you doing, how did you define yourself, and what was important to you at the time? And now think about five years ago, and then ten. You have changed (and will continue to change). So will your North Star.

It grows and evolves with you, which is why it's important to take time often to think about the components of your North Star and ask yourself, *Does it reflect me and where I want to go now?* It's okay if it doesn't. It just means it's time to shake things up a little, or maybe even a lot, like I did when I took the time to redirect my life.

Just take a deep breath and don't overthink it. Here we go.

DOING: YOUR MISSION STATEMENT

Your mission statement answers the question: "What do I do?" It should be true to you and should be specific enough for people to understand what you do and why you do it. A lot of people and companies get this wrong by using big fancy words that don't tell us anything. *Clear and concise* is the name of the game. We want our mission statement to be easy to memorize and repeat because we will be referencing it often.

Here are some examples of mission statements:

AMAZON: To offer our customers the lowest possible prices, the best available selection, and the utmost convenience.

NIKE: To bring inspiration and innovation to every athlete in the world.

PBS: To create content that educates, informs and inspires.

INKWELL PRESS: To provide productivity tools and trainings that empower you to achieve your goals and dreams.

When you think about these companies, do you see how their mission statements allow them to make decisions about their movements and their choices? You'll notice that their statements are not about the *things* they do— Nike doesn't tell you they make athletic gear, and PBS doesn't talk about producing great children's programs. Instead, a mission statement gets to the heart of why they do these things: "to bring inspiration and innovation" or "to create content that educates."

When it comes to your mission statement, maybe the question you should be asking isn't "What do I do?" but it should dig deeper and ask, "*Why* do I do what I do?"

You can see how a mission statement helps these companies determine what they spend their resources on—and what they don't. It allows a large group of people, like the employees of the company, to be empowered to make choices and decisions because they all have a common purpose.

Even though you are one person and not a group, you, too, are inundated by choices. And while you aren't offering a product or service, you are crafting a legacy—that's your ultimate product, the impact you make for yourself and others. We all have gifts; there's a feeling of satisfaction when you focus your time and energy on what is truly at the heart of what you do. Writing a mission statement for yourself gives you that clarity.

Oprah Winfrey's mission is: "To be a teacher. And to be known for inspiring my students to be more than they thought they could be." Richard Branson's mission is: "To have fun in [my] journey through life and learn from mistakes."

My personal mission statement is: "To use my passion and expertise in productivity to inspire others to achieve their goals and dreams." Notice I don't mention the words *business owner* or *author* or *podcaster*. It's a short statement that conveys what I do and why.

One of the beauties of a mission statement is that it helps guide and remind you of what you do, but it doesn't box you in. It provides the framework you use to make your decisions. When it's time for me to decide whether to say yes to a project or whether to join a committee, the proposal must first filter through my mission statement. I ask myself, *Does this fulfill my mission?* If it does, I move forward. My mission, though, doesn't just tell me what to say yes to—it also gives me the fortitude to pass on opportunities that do not fulfill my mission. If something doesn't fit my mission, the answer is a clear and simple no.

Through my mission statement, I was inspired to open inkWELL Press, to start my podcast, to create TonyaTV, and offer courses. You can see how it has given me the insight to know what I really want to focus on every day, but it doesn't limit me either.

I think one of the struggles many people experience with an exercise like this is that it's hard to zero in on one statement. We have so many facets to our lives we cannot imagine a single statement being able to convey it all. What I often end up seeing are extraordinarily long mission statements trying to cover all the many tasks people do. These statements end up sounding more like a laundry list of jobs than a true mission statement, which should say clearly and concisely what you *really* do. I'll give you an example of what I mean by this.

Amanda, an alum of my liveWELL Method course, is a good example of a woman with a lot on her plate. Because of this, it could be hard to narrow down what she does into a single mission statement. After all, she homeschools her three daughters, teaches high school English at her co-op, works part-time as a physical therapist, *and* works on her dream business on the side: being a professional organizer who helps others systemize their homes and business papers. (I told you she had a lot on her plate, didn't I?)

Amanda wears so many hats that she wasn't sure where to laser in on her mission statement, but I noticed a key thread running through each of her activities. She is consistently spreading love and helping others in many different forms. When we focused on the root of *why* she does each of these tasks, she said she is passionate about helping others overcome challenges, "inviting them to walk in hope, empowerment, and freedom." Once she acknowledged this, Amanda was able to create a mission statement she felt reflected her many hats. Her mission statement is: "I use my humor and problem-solving skills to help improve the lives of my family, friends, and community."

Your mission statement isn't about your job itself—it's about what your job does and why you do it. I know that might seem confusing, but here's a simpler way to look at it: Think about all the tasks you truly enjoy, and then start to question what it is about these jobs that brings you joy. Do you see a theme beginning to emerge? Is there a common thread running through each of these tasks? That theme—the reason *why* you do those tasks—that's the heart of your mission statement.

When we understand our *why*, we can answer the question of *what* we do.

So where do you start? Here is one of the simple exercises I used to help create my mission statement. It's called the ABC Brain Dump, and it's one of my favorite exercises to use when I feel like I'm stuck. I list all the letters of the alphabet on a sheet of paper, A to Z. Then I sit for two minutes and think about the question I'm considering. In this case, I asked myself, *Why do I do what I do?*

Then I start writing, starting with A and working my way through the alphabet, one minute for each letter. Don't think, don't filter, just write! After going through all twenty-six letters, I begin to look for words that pop out at me or themes that recur.

I then explore those ideas even further. I may do another brain dump focused just on this new theme, or I'll create a mind map, allowing my brain to run unfiltered while writing out connected ideas.

When you need to flush out an idea, give it the time and space it needs to be uncovered. Don't rush it, but don't give yourself a never-ending deadline. You don't want this to become a vehicle for procrastination. Just allow yourself the space you need to think.

If you're having trouble getting started, here are a couple of questions you can ask yourself: *What am I passionate about? What makes me great? Why do I enjoy what I do?*

DREAMING: YOUR VISION STATEMENT

A vision statement answers the question: "Where am I going?" It's where we dream we will be. This may be very different from where we are right now. It helps set our trajectory and define where the destination lies. While the mission statement tells us where we are today, the vision statement clarifies where we want to be in the future.

A vision statement is not your goals—it's a description of your future that instills hope. It's not the nitty-gritty details of each step required to get there; it's a guideline to help you understand the goals you may need to set. It's not necessarily tied to your current reality—that's one of the best parts of a vision statement. A vision statement is an opportunity to dream and imagine the best possible future.

Some examples of focused vision statements:

MAKE-A-WISH: That people everywhere will share the power of a wish.

AVON: To be the company that best understands and satisfies the product, service and self-fulfillment needs of women—globally.

ASPCA: That the United States is a humane community in which all animals are treated with respect and kindness.

INKWELL PRESS: To help people everywhere live a fulfilling life focusing on their priorities.

Did you notice that all these statements were fewer than twenty words? Like a mission statement, you want your vision statement to be short and direct—one sentence or phrase will do. You want to design it to clearly share what you are working to achieve in a way that is easy to communicate to others.

Did you also notice that all of these are written in absolute terms? You don't see phrases like "hope to be" or "would like to have" included. They are written as if these statements are inevitable; these visions will absolutely come true.

Because vision statements are meant to be used internally, many companies don't publish them for the public to see. Most people follow this as well, since it's really designed to be a more personal statement. I'm happy to share mine, though. My vision statement is: "I will help people everywhere live a fulfilling life, focusing on their priorities while focusing on my own."

One of the most powerful exercises I used when designing my vision statement was to create a vision board. A vision board is a visual representation of the future that you can then use to craft a concise and meaningful vision statement.

Simply gather together a pile of magazines you don't mind cutting up and start flipping. Look for images and words that inspire you. When something jumps out at you, rip it out. And then keep flipping. Don't stop. As you find more images or words that resonate with you, add them to your stack.

Once you have a nice stack, begin to go through them. Intentionally choose images and words representing the vision of the future you want. Attach the images on a large sheet of paper or poster board, something you can hang in a place where you'll see it often. Then use the ideas you've gathered to craft a meaningful vision statement for yourself.

Here are a few questions you can ask yourself to help you get started: *How do I want to evolve and grow? How can I make what I'm doing now even better?*

DEFINING: YOUR CORE VALUES

Core values answer the question: "How will I support the mission and vision statements?" Your core values are a group of words that work in concert to create the essential standards that guide your behavior and shape your decisions.

People often claim to live by their core values, but if our values are open-ended and ambiguous, it's easy to get out of alignment and make bad choices. In other words, it's incredibly hard to actually live by your core values if you don't take the time to articulate them clearly and write them down.

You want to create a set of core values that are inspirational and concrete so they have both meaning and action. They should speak to your passions and help drive the decisions you make. When you follow your personal core values, they will fulfill you and help you focus on the person you want to be. Definitively stating your core values doesn't just help with large decisions; it helps with the seemingly small ones as well.

Here are some examples of core values:

SMITHSONIAN: Excellence, Integrity, Respect, Diversity, Intellectual Freedom, Collaboration

ADIDAS: Performance, Passion, Integrity, Diversity

ADOBE: Genuine, Exceptional, Innovative, Involved

INKWELL PRESS: Harmony, Intention, Family, Love, Generosity, Excellence

The values listed for each of these examples reflect how the mission and vision statements will be executed. I've also listed the mission, vision, and core values for inkWELL Press in this chapter so you can see that they seamlessly support each other and work together. Your set of core values will do that too.

My personal core values are Family, Grace, Mindfulness, Learning,

Integrity, and Adventure. You'll notice that for me, as the owner of inkWELL Press, many of my own values overlap with the company's values just as our missions and visions overlap.

I've developed an easy three-step process to make it easier to discover your core values.

1. Reflect + Collect

I often say you need to look *backward* to keep moving *forward*. I believe this is true because the bread crumbs of our lives have led us to where we are at this very moment. Begin thinking about the mission and vision statements you hold true, and then take the time to think back to why these statements embody you.

> **ASK YOURSELF:** What words do I want others to use to describe me when I'm not around? What do I do to impact others in a positive way? Is there a gap between what I'm currently doing and what I'm dreaming of doing?

Start collecting the values that come to mind. It may help to look at a list of common words used for core values—I have a list you can use at joyofmissingout.com/corevalues. Use a highlighter to go through the list, and don't overthink it. Simply highlight the words you feel reflect your values. Don't fret about how many; just allow yourself the freedom to openly choose what resonates with you.

2. Refine + Define

You will at this point have a good-size list of values, but you don't want too many because *when we are so busy trying to do everything, we end up standing for nothing*. I believe six or fewer is a good rule of thumb here: enough to stand for something, but not so many you feel like you're juggling chain saws.

Now you'll want to refine your list, so start looking for ways you can group the words together into categories or themes. For example, when I was doing this exercise for myself, I grouped together words like *authentic, generosity, kindness, thoughtfulness,* and *charity* because they all embodied a similar idea. Once you group your words into categories, choose a name that embodies the full idea. For my group of words, I ended up naming that value "Grace."

Once you have refined your words into these categories, you need to define what these values mean to you. For me, the value of Grace means I believe the single act of a kind gesture can make a stranger's day; a nice comment or compliment has the power to transform. Words are different to each of us, with their own meanings and connotations, so taking the time to spell out exactly what each value means helps clarify it even further.

3. Believe + Achieve

The last step is to begin embodying these values in your daily life. Test the values and make sure they resonate with the mission and vision statements you've created for yourself. Ask yourself, *Would I stick to this core value even if it created a disadvantage? Does this fit into my personality?*

Let me explain what I mean by this—a good example is the value of *innovation.* It's a wonderful value, but if you are a person who thrives on stability, the constant change of innovation may not work for you. A good rule of thumb is to ask yourself: *Am I willing to sacrifice for my value?* If not, it's not the value for you. And that's okay.

———

Sherry, one of my podcast listeners, felt unsure about her life's direction. While working through these exercises, she discovered that some of her happiest moments were times when she was outdoors. When she discovered this, she also realized that most of her daily activities were keeping her confined inside. Armed with her newfound value of "Outdoor Adventures," she was able to create a life that consistently gave her reasons to spend time outside, which increased her overall happiness.

Start actively working to incorporate your values into your daily life and intentionally making them a part of your decision making. If you live a life focused on your values, people will see them and know them without you needing to point them out. They will see them from the actions you take, the words you speak, and the life you lead. Your core values fulfill the prophecy of your mission and vision statements and create structure for the life you want to live.

YOUR NORTH STAR MATTERS

After his cancer diagnosis, Steve Jobs said, "Remembering that I'll be dead soon is the most important tool I've ever encountered to help me make the big choices in life." We don't have to wait until we receive bad news from the doctor or read our obituary in the paper. We can begin to make those big choices now, using our North Star to help guide us.

When we design a life where our mission, vision, and core values are an integral part, we have a guide to help us with the overwhelm we may have been feeling. A good North Star guides you to know what decisions to make and how to start.

The process of defining your North Star might seem daunting, but the important thing to remember is not to be scared. *You can't mess this up.* If you find you're not happy with the parts that make up your North Star, simply adjust it—just as I did, just as Alfred Nobel did. This is *your* North Star, and it needs to add meaning and value to *your* life.

 ### LET ME HELP

I know it's hard to start when a blank page is staring back at you. Don't worry. I've got a free exercise for you to work through that is designed to be a springboard for discovering your own North Star. It's not any ordinary download, though; it's an interactive exercise with an activity and a video so I can guide you through the process. You can get free access to this bonus feature at joyofmissingout.com/chapter3.

FIND CLARITY

 2

Clarify how to choose the projects or tasks that will have the most impact on your goals and priorities.

In the next step of the liveWELL Method, we will build upon the unique priorities you discovered in section 1 so they sit front and center every day. Let's think about how we are spending our three resources of time, energy, and focus. The following chapters explore each of these elements, clarifying how we can use each to its fullest potential, which allows us to spend our days on what matters most.

Together we will work to shift your mindset so that you understand why you want to stop working on being efficient, why you want to "burn your boats," and ultimately how you can prioritize your priorities. You will learn a simple framework to help discern the important from the unimportant so you know where to spend your time, energy, and focus. My goal as we work through these chapters is to help you establish how you can ensure that your "first things" come first.

CHAPTER 4

CLARIFY FOCUS

*Don't spend time beating on a wall, hoping
to transform it into a door.*
COCO CHANEL

*It's the end of the day and I feel worn thin like an old T-shirt. I'm
quick to snap at John and the kids because I am so busy fighting
off the tears of frustration that I don't have any more of me to give.
I don't even have time to sit down. I keep working, I keep pushing
forward, pretending to be happy when all the while I wonder, Why?
Why is life like this, where I feel so caught up in the current that I
can barely breathe? I feel like I've got to hold it together; I cannot let
them see me fail. The pressure of holding it together is making me
anxious and irritable.*

*I wake up in the morning feeling like I'm already behind. There's
no time to linger under the warm sheets because I feel like my day has
already slipped out of my grasp and I'm scrambling to keep up.*

I found this rambling scribbled on a piece of paper wedged like a book-
mark in an old book I was rereading. The edges of the paper were smooth

and flat like the pressed four-leaf clovers in my family Bible and the word *cannot* was underlined so many times the page had torn slightly under the weight of my frustration. I took a minute to read over this fragment of my former life, and I wondered what day I had written it. Was it on a hot Tuesday in the middle of July or a cool Sunday early in March?

There's honestly no telling because at that point in my life I was pin-balling from task to task throughout my day, with no true direction. I kept myself busy, filling my day with tasks that felt so important at the time, but now I can barely remember a single one. I was living my days in a constant state of not knowing where to focus.

I worried about saying no, I fretted about keeping up appearances, and I stressed that I wasn't doing enough—even though I was running myself ragged. I was afraid to miss out on any opportunities, so I was saying yes to anything and everything. My attention was scattered like leaves in a windstorm. I didn't know it at the time, but I needed to discover the joy that comes when we center our lives on what is truly important and learn to let go of the rest.

TOO MUCH IS SOMETIMES JUST TOO MUCH

For too long, I had no idea where to spend my time or how to spend my energy. I wasn't productive—I was simply running around being busy, filling my days but not my soul. I was lacking focus, one of the three key elements of true productivity that allows us to choose how we spend our day.

To be genuinely productive, we must master our focus. That can feel difficult, though, I know. We are pulled in a thousand different directions through the pings on our phones, the blips of our inbox, and the endless opportunities we have before us. In our digital age, we have more information at our fingertips than ever before in history. We have watches that tell us our heart rate and apps that tell us precisely what time we should expect rain this evening. We have alerts on our phones to tell us about traffic and more access to news than we ever even thought we wanted.

It seems like this abundance of information should make life easier, but when we are bombarded with so much of it, the paradox is that decision making becomes more difficult. This is when the feeling of overwhelm begins to settle in and we simply don't know where to start.

It's been estimated that we receive approximately 11 million pieces of information every second from our nerve endings, but our brains can only process a mere forty bits. In his book *Smarter Faster Better*, Charles Duhigg referred to this phenomenon as information blindness. He wrote, "Just as snow blindness refers to people losing the capacity to distinguish trees from hills under a blanket of powder, so information blindness refers to our mind's tendency to stop absorbing data when there's too much to take in." In other words, it's like processing a few snowflakes in the midst of a blizzard. There seems to be no easy way to wade through the information and choose where to focus, so our natural reaction is simply to stop filtering. We choose not to choose.

We have to become comfortable with some doubt because oftentimes the problem isn't discerning between good and bad—the black and white—it's choosing between two good choices. It's when the black and white blends into gray. It's the good, better, and best—how do you decide where to focus? I hear you.

I received a letter from Amanda in Salem, South Dakota, who described this dilemma well:

> I have all these thoughts and ideas . . . but I STRUGGLE in the action portion, I feel like this massive paralysis comes over me when I actually need to put ideas to work. I feel like I don't know where to start in getting my life organized to better enjoy my family and work.

Amanda is not alone in feeling this way—and neither are you.

WE WANT TO BURN THE BOATS

Archimedes was a Greek mathematician and inventor in ancient Syracuse. There are many anecdotes about Archimedes, but the legend of his defense of his hometown against the onslaught of conquering Romans is one of my favorites.

Archimedes knew his countrymen were far outnumbered and did not have the sophisticated weaponry needed to defend their coast, so he devised a simple weapon constructed solely of mirrors, which he placed high on the cliffs. This effective tool did one job: it reflected the rays of the sun. Directing the rays toward the oncoming boats, he was able to ignite every enemy ship before it reached the shoreline, keeping his country safe. What's important to note is that it wasn't the sun alone that protected the coast—it was the focus of the sun's energy.

As Alexander Graham Bell once said, "Concentrate all your thought upon the work at hand. The sun's rays do not burn until brought to a focus." It's not about creating a huge effort; it's about focusing like a magnifying glass in order to burn the boats.

One way to help ignite that fire is by setting goals. Similar to Archimedes's mirror, goals focus our energy into a powerful motivator. Goals, when done correctly, are the magnifying glass we need to concentrate our energy and sharpen our focus. They help us weed through all the information and center in on the steps we want to take to move ourselves forward.

This is key in moving us along the path our North Star is guiding us toward. Goals are an extension of the foundation we have created, and they help shape our choices to get us to the end result we want.

If you are anything like most people, you may find yourself questioning whether goal setting really works (especially if it hasn't for you in the past), but I'll share a study that shows the power of setting goals.

Researchers studied Harvard MBA students before graduation and asked them, "Have you set clear, written goals for your future and made plans to accomplish them?" They found that 84 percent of students had no goals set, 13 percent had goals in mind but didn't write them down, and only 3 percent had goals written on paper along with clear plans to accomplish them.

Ten years passed, and the researchers checked back in with the graduates and discovered that the abstract goal setters were making twice the amount of money as the students who had set no goals. Impressive, right? But the real success story was in the 3 percent who had written their goals; they were taking home ten times the amount of the other 97 percent *combined*.

Why does setting goals help? Because it helps us clarify what we want to accomplish. In other words, it tells us where to focus. It enables us to clearly see the path we want to take and triggers our behavior. When we set a goal, it naturally directs our focus to where we want to expend our energy and our time.

Without goals, how do you know the trajectory of your path? Goals tell us exactly where to aim. As Zig Ziglar said, "If you aim at nothing, you'll hit it every time." We don't want to hit nothing, do we? No. We have the power to burn boats if we stay focused.

When we lose focus on our priorities, we are simply along for the ride, going wherever the day takes us. The act of focusing is that—an act. It's a verb rather than a noun. And this focus requires making choices. Choices may feel difficult, because when we eliminate options and "miss out" on purpose, we feel that we are limiting ourselves, but in reality, that's what allows us the freedom to live the life we really want.

SETTING BOUNDARIES OPENS NEW POSSIBILITIES

We have to cut in order to really grow and flourish. I know this seems counterintuitive, but think of a garden: Do you plant the flowers one on top of another? Do you squeeze so many in that there is no room? Or do you allow each plant to have space—space to receive the rain and the sun, space to spread their leaves and grow? That's what we need: space to allow ourselves to focus. The only way to have that space is to actively create it for ourselves. We need boundaries.

Often we hear a word like *boundaries* and believe that we are limiting ourselves and our choices. What we don't realize is that boundaries are actually a source of freedom. Solid boundaries allow us that space we need to focus.

Some time ago I heard an example about boundaries that helped put all the puzzle pieces in place for me. I want to share it in hopes that it does the same for you. Imagine a school nestled close to a busy road. When the children go out for recess, they have to stay close by the building where the teachers can keep them safe. But if the very same school were to build a fence—a boundary—surrounding the playground, what would happen then? The children would be free to run and play. The options for kickball and playful games of tag would open up for them. The boundaries would give them the freedom to explore and move.

That's what we need in our lives too—not a fence to protect us from fast-moving cars maybe, but clear compartments that allow us the freedom to dive deeper, explore, and focus.

When we compartmentalize, we give ourselves that space and freedom. In the first section of the book, I talked about the three buckets in our lives: work, home, and personal. Creating boundaries allows you to focus on each area within its own time so that each is treated as a priority in its dedicated space.

The time we spend doesn't need to be perfectly equal for each. Sometimes we want to spend more time in one compartment than another. Remember, it's not about balance—balance doesn't exist—it's all about creating harmony.

Each compartment is a part of our whole selves, but when we allow the parts to exist separately, we are able to focus completely on each, giving it the space it deserves. Each one receives the priority treatment. As we move through our day, we close one compartment and open the next one—like a door we close behind us before we open the one ahead. It's important to note that it's not a revolving door—I firmly shut one in my mind before I open the next. For me, when I leave the office I'm shutting the door to my work compartment behind me and I'm opening up the one to my personal compartment. This allows me to be fully present and available for my family, giving them the focus they deserve.

I know this can be a challenge—we all are tempted to crack open a compartment just slightly, like a quick check of our work email while chatting with our spouse. But what's the message we are sending?

Sometimes we are our own worst distraction.

You know what I'm talking about—we've all done it. We check our email on our phone, see nothing there, and then inexplicably check it again two minutes later. Did we expect something to change in there? Or the bigger question is, what *do* we expect to see in there? One study found that one in three people claimed to check their email every fifteen minutes, but in reality they were checking every five minutes! This means we are constantly interrupting ourselves and we're not even aware of it.

We have to stop checking our email incessantly, like we're hunting for a prize at the bottom of the cereal box when we know there's really nothing more than cereal there. I don't know about your inbox, but mine is more like Grape-Nuts than Lucky Charms—not a ton of fun and excitement to be had in reality!

It's not as simple as blaming technology, though; this tendency is actually hardwired into our DNA. According to that same study, most people who check email every five minutes are not receiving any sort of alert—they are simply feeling the pull to check in. Our brains are designed to constantly scan for new information, which was great for our cave-dwelling ancestors who were always on the lookout for food, water, and predators. But it's not helpful for us in today's digital world where distractions are everywhere. In fact, researchers estimate that workers are interrupted every eleven minutes on average. Distractions take almost twenty-five minutes to recover from, so most people spend about one-third of their day trying to get back to their deep work.

So how can we focus in today's 24-7 culture? How can we possibly get to the deep work? The ability to focus seems like a luxury, but it's not—it's essential to true productivity.

When we create strong borders around our time, we are able to become the best we can be. Think about it. When you are at work, you are a business-person. When you are not, you play all the other roles: wife, mother, best friend, aunt, neighbor. Give each role in your life the opportunity to shine. Boundaries allow you to do that.

When we don't clearly stake our boundaries, we end up being overrun by the demands others put on us. And to be honest with you, it's not really their fault. If we don't communicate our boundaries, how do others know when they've crossed them?

CLEAR AND DIRECT COMMUNICATION

I walk to the front of the room and carefully select one folded sheet of paper from the bowl. As I unfold it, I see the words *Peter Pan* scrawled in black ink. Relief fills my body and a smile creeps across my face. *Simple,* I think. *They'll guess this in no time and we will be crowned the charades champions.* In my family, winning charades is a time-cherished honor, establishing bragging rights for the rest of the holiday weekend. We must get this right.

I walk with confidence to the center of the room and make the gesture to indicate it's a book. I laugh to myself because this is just going to be too easy. I stand with my feet apart, my chest expanded, and place both hands on my hips—you know, Peter Pan style.

And they shout, "Wonder Woman." *Really?* So I shake my head no, but still they repeat, "Wonder Woman!" I am being crystal clear—*How can they not know I'm Peter Pan? This is so obvious!* I shake my head emphatically again, certain they will get it right. But they are already off and running, calling out comic book characters.

And there I stand, with hands on my hips, wondering how in the world we got to Spider-Man when I'm clearly Peter Pan, not Peter Parker.

It's frustrating when we feel we are telling people what we want but they just don't get it. Isn't it? But that's the trouble with boundaries. We think we've created boundaries for ourselves, but we don't accurately communicate what we want. We get frustrated when we find that people have invaded our sacred spaces. They expect emails at eight o'clock at night or phone calls on the weekend, but because we have not clearly set our borders, it's not their fault our boundaries have been crossed. It's ours—we have to make sure we communicate them. But just as I discussed in section 1, our stories may be telling us that it's rude or selfish to clearly define our borders.

Allow me to sprinkle a little truth on you here: being kind and being assertive are not mutually exclusive. We are allowing our old stories to tell us that we don't have the right to our own time.

If we are constantly answering emails, texts, and calls from others, no matter the time, we are setting an expectation. Without meaning to, we are communicating to others that we are always available. All it really takes is a little gentle training. Set boundaries with work and family so your work knows when you're spending time with family and your friends and family know when you're focused at work.

Let your work team know that you won't be responding to email immediately when it's outside of work hours. Many of us do feel the need to check in after hours, and that's okay. We just don't need to be at the beck and call of our business at every hour of the day. We can set aside a block of time to intentionally check in with work after hours; just make sure you don't leave that block open-ended. Set a start time *and an end time* for you to jump back into that work compartment.

The same holds true for friends and family while you are at work. It's important for them to respect that boundary as well. After all, you can't tell your boss not to call you while you are on vacation if you spend half your workday on personal calls.

My best friend never calls me during the workday, and I don't call her. We allow each other to focus on our work, which then allows us to fully enjoy each other (and our families) during our personal time. Because we have this mutual respect for our boundaries, we know that when we are spending time with each other, we aren't also trying to read an email or squeeze in a work task. We are both fully focused on our conversation, making it more meaningful. Separating my compartments allows me to give each the attention it deserves.

I know this might feel difficult to do, especially if you don't work at a traditional office. Maybe you work from home or run your own business,

BEING KIND *and*
BEING ASSERTIVE
ARE NOT *mutually* EXCLUSIVE

so people think that you don't have set hours—this is when it's even more important to set up these compartments and clearly define them. Yes, it may take a few gentle reminders, but I promise you, they will get the message.

Your kids can also be taught to allow you to focus. Listen, if people can train a monkey to ride a tricycle, then your kids can be trained too. I taught my kids at a young age the sound of my work ringtone, and when they heard it they knew that was their cue to quiet down and allow me to talk on the phone. When I tell people this, they seem amazed that a four-year-old could do it, but have you ever seen preschoolers during a fire drill? They line up quietly and follow directions.

Do preschoolers know to do this right away? Absolutely not—they've been trained. As a former teacher, I just use the tricks I learned in the classroom—like doing pretend practice runs and rehearsals, acting out different scenarios, and giving my kids options and choices so they feel empowered to know what to do while I'm on my call. I made training fun so my kids thought we were playing a game, but they were learning.

We found ways to make boundaries work and you can, too, but you have to communicate. You have to set expectations and follow through. Kids can be a big asset to your productivity if you allow them to be.

BUT THAT DOESN'T WORK IN THE REAL WORLD

I can see the critics already—their mouths open, ready to argue that there's no way setting boundaries works in a typical workplace. But it does. Standing tall and staking your boundaries at work requires courage, but it's the only way to effect the changes you need.

———

I first met Jordan through the nonprofit where she works. With a ready smile and a beautiful laugh, she is generous and thoughtful. She has spent the majority of her life pushing forward causes she believes in and working tirelessly to improve the lives of others.

Jordan was excited to sign up for the liveWELL Method course, but when I started to talk about boundaries at work, she thought, *That's all fine and good if you work for yourself and can set it up. How does that work, though, if I'm not the one in control of my calendar? I work for a nonprofit that's always rapidly innovating as we go. I'm always in a place of doing urgent tasks and don't see that ever changing.*

With big donors and a leadership team that works tirelessly, it's easy to tell ourselves the story that this is impossible: our bosses won't allow it; our workflows are fixed and can't be changed. But Jordan humored me (those are her own words) and took a look at her typical day.

She opted to block off the first two hours of her day on her shared calendar to focus on deeper work. She also decided that she would not check email until after her block was finished, because she felt that her inbox had the power to lead her astray, affecting the flow of her day and her mood. She liked the idea of a series of small wins first thing in her day—but didn't think the strategy would really work. *It's a pipe dream,* she thought.

Here's what Jordan says today:

Because people have access to my calendar, they will discuss it with me if they need to meet during my focused time. Because it's blocked, though, they often don't ask—they schedule around it. And now, I'm far more able to conquer what's important to me. I'm getting to be more strategic.

I've also come to realize my important work is also important to others. I am living my values beyond my working life. I remember before my first child, my whole identity was tied to work, but after I became a mom it felt confusing—I didn't want work to be my only role. By setting my compartments, I'm able to tell myself at five o'clock that work time is over. With a five-year-old who goes to bed at 7:00 p.m., that time is precious. I would miss most of my evening with him if I didn't set my boundaries. That's time I want to spend with him.

Did you notice the words I did? *Conquer. Strategic. Values.*

The other benefit Jordan has experienced through boundaries? She ends her day with a full marble jar. She shared, "I can really see the good I've done. In putting boundaries in place and getting those small wins with one or two projects out the door before checking email, I can better acknowledge myself. I get to focus in, do meaningful work, and feel satisfied with what I got accomplished. It's amazing how one small change can have a ripple effect—simply adding that two-hour morning block to my time has helped me find harmony."

Was there pushback? When Jordan first shared her plans with a co-worker, she heard the response, "But as a nonprofit, we're in the business of customer service!" Jordan, though, set her boundaries and replied, "Our donors are going to get a much better response from me if I'm purposely carving out my time to address their needs. Having boundaries allows me to be more effective."

Her productivity boost is working, and it's showing in her work. She's now noticing that others on her team are starting to do the same with their schedules.

I often hear the excuse, "I don't own my time." But you do. We just feel guilty doing it, as if we don't have a right to our own calendar.

Researcher Brené Brown has discovered that "the clearer and more respected our boundaries, the higher the level of empathy and compassion for others. Fewer clear boundaries, less openness. It's hard to stay kindhearted when you feel people are taking advantage of you." And I couldn't agree more. Work becomes a happier place each day when you feel you can conquer what's important.

There's no need for us to spin around like a top, feeling so uncertain, as I used to do. When we have clear boundaries in place, we are able to focus our time and our energy so we can be more present for our priorities. Stop spinning and start living.

CHAPTER 5

CLARIFY TIME

Perfectionism is just fear in fancy shoes and a mink coat.
ELIZABETH GILBERT

I had just finished speaking to a crowded room of entrepreneurs and was making my way off the stage when a striking brunette cut in front of my path. I looked at her and smiled, and she gave me a quick, nervous smile back. "I loved your keynote," she said, "and I love the idea of this priority-centered life in work and at home, but is it really possible?" I looked her in the eye and asked her the question I've asked a thousand women before her: "What do you think is holding you back from living your best life?" And without hesitation, she responded, "Time."

What she didn't realize at that moment was that I already knew her answer. It's almost always the same. *Time.* Again and again I find that people believe they need more time in order to live the life they really want. But they are wrong.

We cannot gain more time. We all have the same 168 hours in our week—there's no changing that. Productivity isn't a magical Time-Turner around Hermione's neck. We simply cannot give someone more time. What we can do, though, is change our mindset on how we spend our time and where we focus our energy.

We wield the power over time, not the other way around.

To do this, though, we have to begin to challenge the idea of #allthethings. We don't need to do more. We just need to rethink busy and work toward true productivity: spending our time on what matters most—the people, the tasks, our purpose—those priorities we discovered in section 1.

When we have this mindset, when our eyes are fully open, the possibilities become endless.

WE WANT TO BE EFFICIENT, DON'T WE?

We need to change the way we think about being productive. We believe that we need to be efficient, to try to get as many tasks done in as little time as possible. We cram our day full with one task after the other in a mad dash to win the day. You know what I'm talking about. We've all seen the clickbait articles promising you can write a year's worth of blog content in three days or fooling you into believing you can write a book in a week.

Hurry, hurry, rush, rush. No time for lunch. No time to stop. Quickly moving from one task to the next with the goal of checking off as many tasks from our list as we can in as little time as possible. Being efficient.

Are we stopping to ask ourselves, though, if those tasks need to be done at all? Are those things we are hurrying to do really important? Or are we just mindlessly rushing through our to-do list, pinballing from one item to the next, exhausting ourselves? This is why we slip into bed and feel as though we didn't do enough or get enough done, that we weren't good enough even when we skipped lunch and did five tasks at the same time. *Enough.*

We are so busy working to be efficient that we don't have the time to catch our breath and ask ourselves the most important question of all: *Why?* Why are these tasks on our list? Why do they need to be done? Why are we killing ourselves to do it all?

Productivity isn't about being efficient—it's not about filling our day with tasks to quickly check off. It's about being *effective* and asking yourself if those tasks need to be done at all. I want to remind you: productivity is not getting more done—it's focusing on what matters most.

Dishwashers are efficient; refrigerators are efficient. They are working hard with the least amount of resources and effort. And that is possible because they are machines—machines designed to do one thing over and over again: dishwashers clean plates, and refrigerators keep things cool.

Unfortunately, when people focus on being efficient, the resource we target is time. We fail to realize that *being efficient is about getting things done; being effective is getting what's important done.* There's a big difference.

EFFICIENT	EFFECTIVE
DEADLINE FOCUSED	GOAL FOCUSED
THINKING OF THE PRESENT	THINKING OF THE FUTURE
DOING MORE IN LESS TIME	DOING MORE QUALITY WORK

Here is an example of what I mean: At 10:00 a.m., you ask an assistant to send out a project by 4:00 p.m. The *efficient* assistant rushes to get it done, her mind fixed on the time. She works through lunch and sends it out by the time you requested. It's not proofread or fact-checked, but she's met her deadline.

The *effective* assistant takes the assignment and creates a plan. She breaks down the steps to accomplish the task and prioritizes the work so everything is done to the best of her ability. She realizes the 4:00 p.m. deadline can't be achieved and meets with you to adjust the goals. Together you decide it's better to send it out at 4:30 p.m. so it can be beautifully designed, proofread, and fact-checked. The project goes out and is exactly the type of quality work you want to reflect you.

Remember, efficiency is doing a lot of work; effectiveness is doing the *important* work. Quality wins every time. And yes, we want to use less energy and time, but not at the expense of quality. Sometimes we are so caught up in deadlines, we don't realize that the processes we believe make us faster are working against us. I call these the three myths of productivity.

MYTH 1: I'M AN EXCELLENT MULTITASKER

We take a lot of pride in our multitasking abilities, don't we? We mention it casually in job interviews, dropping it in the conversation like a beautiful shiny star. We mention it because it's a badge of honor, evidence of our ninja-like productivity prowess.

I used to feel that way, too, until I took the time to understand *why* multitasking was actually working against me.

A lot of what we call multitasking is really switch-tasking: simultaneously performing two tasks at the same time, switching from one task to another and performing two or more tasks in rapid succession. The problem is, our brains are not designed to work that way; each section is designed to do one task at a time—like a lightbulb turning on and off.

The executive system of your brain sits above your eyes and works like a conductor of an orchestra, switching the sections on and off. For example, if you are watching TV and someone is having a conversation in the room, the conductor may direct the brain to prioritize the pictures on the screen and turn down the conversation.

This switching quickly from one task to the next is causing our brains to work harder than necessary, and this cognitive cost adds up. *Scientists have discovered that when we multitask, our productivity actually decreases by as much as 40 percent.* Yes, decreases. That's about sixteen hours we lose every week when we multitask.

It's not just the time that suffers either. In a University of London study, researchers found that while people multitasked, their IQs dropped to levels similar to what we might find in someone who skipped a night of sleep or smoked marijuana. Yes, you read that right. When we multitask, we are not working smarter, we are working—well, you get the idea.

I know what you are thinking. You are thinking it might be true for some people but not for you. And, yes, a very small number of people excel at doing two or more things at once—but it's only a mere 2 percent of the population. These people are referred to as "supertaskers."

The irony is that when people learn these rare exceptions exist, they run with that fact as evidence that they, too, are the exception. But "they are not," David Strayer, the head researcher at the University of Utah, bluntly stated. "The ninety-eight percent of us, we deceive ourselves. And we tend to overrate our ability to multitask." In fact, when Strayer took his research a step further, he uncovered another strong relationship—an inverse one. The better someone believed she was at multitasking, the worse her abilities were.

Why do we feel obligated to multitask? We think it makes us faster, but we know from those studies I just shared that not only is multitasking taking us longer, but it's also causing the quality of our work to suffer. We are doing our work half as well and taking twice as long—all while stressing ourselves out. That doesn't seem effective, does it?

When I posed this question to some of the students in my course, one woman admitted:

> If I am being honest, I think I multitask and get things done for a few reasons. I am very committed to seeing things through. . . . I don't want people to question my work, so maybe part of it is a need to prove I can do it all (and well) . . . proving my worth. Also, if I am focusing on "all the things," I don't have to dig deeper and get to the messy, vulnerable stuff.

I love the honesty she shared. I want to ask you if you think this is true for you. Do you pile more onto yourself, stressing yourself out, because you feel you have to prove your worth? Is it to keep yourself busy?

We want people to think we are good enough—that we deserve the praise, the job, all the good. Why do we feel the need to prove it?

MYTH 2: I DON'T HAVE TIME TO TAKE A BREAK

One common technique we use is to muscle through projects even when we feel tired or sluggish. We are so busy racing the clock that we don't realize our brains need time to rest.

The entire universe is dictated by rhythms: the rising and setting of the sun, the ebb and flow of the tides, the movement between seasons. All organisms, including humans, follow rhythms whether we realize it or not.

You've probably heard of your circadian rhythm, which is the 24-hour internal clock all living beings use to regulate eating and sleeping. That's what tells us to be awake for 16 hours and then asleep for 8 hours. Within the circadian rhythm, though, lives our ultradian rhythm, a shorter biological cycle of 90 to 120 minutes that repeats throughout the day.

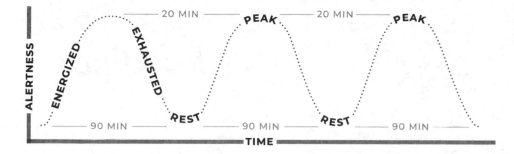

During the first part of the ultradian rhythm, our alertness and brain-wave activity increase, making us feel energized and focused. After about 90 minutes, though, our brains begin to crave rest and renewal. Our brain requires about 20 minutes between each cycle to recover. In other words, the time we use to unplug is a key part of our day—not a frivolous break. We need to understand that periods of rest are not a reward for great work but are a requirement for great work to happen.

As Zen priest and Buddhist teacher Joan Halifax shared, "There is the in-breath and there is the out-breath, and it's easy to believe that we must exhale all the time without ever inhaling. But the inhale is absolutely essential if you want to continue to exhale."

PERIODS OF REST
ARE NOT A *reward* FOR GREAT WORK
BUT ARE A REQUIREMENT FOR
GREAT WORK *to happen*

We cannot work solidly for long blocks of time—our bodies simply don't work that way. And if we are insisting on blocking off a solid three- or four-hour power session, we really aren't doing more work; we are just wearing our brains out.

We don't typically think of work like this—as "on" or "off"—because we feel the need to push ourselves to work harder and longer. But that actually doesn't add to our productivity. In most cases, working more hours is detrimental to the work we create.

Stanford researchers discovered that your productivity actually drops dramatically once you hit the 50-hour mark in your workweek. Workers who put in 70 hours produce nothing more with those extra 20 hours. They are simply spinning their wheels, working longer but accomplishing less. It's not about the time you put in; it's the quality of that time.

While the studies I shared are new, the concept isn't. In 1914 Henry Ford took the industry-shaking steps of doubling his workers' wages and cutting shifts from nine hours to eight. He had dozens of years of research to back up his radical steps, but he still received criticism from the industry—until they all saw how this increased Ford's output (and then began implementing the steps themselves).

Even people who love to work (and I count myself among them) are not performing at high levels once they get to a certain point. Once we understand and begin to work within our natural rhythms, we'll find we work more effectively, creating higher quality with less effort.

Patty, a member of my Facebook group, shared this breakthrough:

> I am a night owl and always feel more productive at night. (Definitely NOT a morning person.) I try to fall asleep at 10, and I just keep tossing and turning and checking my phone. But lately, instead of fighting it completely, I've started taking advantage of my natural rhythm, while also attempting to get my 7 hours of sleep. I started a night cleaning routine and get much more done in 2 hours at night than I get done all day.
>
> My son is an early riser, so I placed breakfast in an accessible spot in the fridge so he can dress and feed himself when he's hungry in the

morning, and I get to wake up refreshed and not rushed. . . . I feel that going with my rhythm and not fighting it has been eye-opening!

Using some Squirrel Strategy and working within our natural rhythms helps us be more effective.

MYTH 3: TECHNOLOGY IS ALWAYS BETTER

One common misconception is the belief that technology is necessary to do everything better, but it's simply not true. Technology is faster and sleeker, but it may surprise you to learn that writing down your ideas and plans on paper is more effective.

Bear with me as we don our lab coats for a minute and take a look at how our brains work. When we pick up a pen, our brain reacts differently than when we are tapping away on a keyboard. Writing triggers the reticular activating system (RAS), which signals our brain to pay attention.

As I mentioned in chapter 4, our brains are constantly bombarded with data. Our RAS is the filter that evaluates what information comes through. It's what wakes us up in the middle of a deep sleep when our babies cry or allows us to hear our own name in a crowded room. It tells our brains where to focus.

Writing triggers your RAS to tell the brain to stay alert—the information is important and needs to be saved where it can be accessed in the future. Typing, on the other hand, does not engage your RAS, so notes and plans tapped into a keyboard are more easily forgotten.

A joint study between Princeton and UCLA discovered that people who took notes with pens performed twice as well on tests as those using laptops. Knowing the laptop users had taken twice as many notes as those who had taken notes by hand, researchers had assumed computer users would be the clear victors. Taking notes on a computer *is* much more efficient, but it's not as effective. And that's the difference.

Don't get me wrong. Technology does need to play a key role in our days. I know it does in mine—even though I'm an advocate of paper planning. Technology is integral for team projects and communication, but we often feel obligated to use it for *all* of our work. We worry that using paper may make us look antiquated, but unplugging can really help our brains see problems in a different light.

Not only does paper engage your brain differently, but because it is more open-ended and flexible, it allows you to reframe thoughts and mold ideas in a way that ingrains the information. This flexibility pushes your brain to actually process and reframe data, deepening the brain's understanding.

———

Rachel* was going through a stressful time in her marriage. She and her husband just couldn't seem to figure out why their relationship was struggling. Rachel had been using one of my paper planners, and in desperation, one afternoon she flipped through the pages to see if she could find some clues as to why her marriage had started to flounder.

> As I went through [my planner] it became very clear to me why we were having marriage problems. You know you get so immersed in your day-to-day life you sometimes forget what happened six months ago. But because I was able to look back . . . that gave the telltale signs of how much stress we were under and the impact it had on our relationship. . . . As I looked over my year and remembered the two [family] deaths, taking on the estate, plus our current business, plus everything else . . . the last sixteen months have been . . . insane. . . . Because I was able to look back at everything and uncover all the culprits, my husband and I were able to talk about this at length, and [I feel] a huge sense of relief.

Writing on paper deepens the relationship between the information and your brain, and it creates the ability for you to see your bread crumbs to help uncover patterns. It allows you to see the bigger picture, which can

———

* Name has been changed.

sometimes feel abstract—it helps you uncover what's important, which is where you really want to spend your time.

WHERE SHOULD WE SPEND OUR TIME?

Effectiveness comes down to priorities. It's the red thread you'll see again and again woven throughout this book. Instead of focusing on trying to do everything, which leaves you feeling like you are herding cats, laser in on the important. The Pareto Principle will help you do that.

The Pareto Principle was introduced in the late 1700s by Vilfredo Pareto, who discovered that 20 percent of our efforts produce 80 percent of our results. The principle applies to all areas—most things in life are not evenly distributed. It's not just a theory. For centuries this principle has been proven time and time again in all areas of life. You've probably heard it called the 80/20 rule:

20 percent of a meeting gives you 80 percent of the information
20 percent of your wardrobe is what you wear 80 percent of the time
20 percent of the people on your team do 80 percent of the work

In other words, all things are not equal and therefore should not be treated as equal.

FOCUS　　　IMPACT

The ratio isn't perfect—it's not always right on the money at a perfect 80/20 split. Warren Buffett attributes 90 percent of his wealth to ten of the companies he invested in. Again and again it's been proven that when you focus on less, you actually achieve more. *It's focused time that creates the greatest impact.* It's not doing more—it's doing what's most important. (Sound familiar?)

If it's been proven that the majority of our success will come from the minority of our tasks, why are we trying to do everything? Shouldn't we be giving the important tasks the larger portion of our time? If we focus on the top 20 percent of our customers and clients, we'll see our sales rise. That's not to say we ignore the other 80 percent, but the top 20 should be getting the lion's share of our attention.

Instead, we often allow the minutia to take over our day . . . the irritable client who definitely doesn't account for 80 percent of our business but wants an hour-long phone call every other day, or the projects that drag out endlessly with no finish line in sight. We have to limit the time we give these items so we can focus on the truly important.

TIME IS LIKE A BOWL OF ICE CREAM

We've all heard the saying "Life is like a box of chocolates," but did you know time is like a bowl of ice cream? I'll tell you what I mean. If you head to your kitchen right now and grab a small bowl and fill it with ice cream, odds are you'll enjoy every single bite. But what if, while rummaging through your cupboard, you find a bigger bowl and fill *this* bowl with ice cream? Will you eat a few bites and put it away? Or will you eat until your spoon scrapes the bottom of the bowl, grabbing those last few melted bits of your Cherry Garcia?

Yep. Me too. No matter which bowl I choose, I will end up eating the amount of ice cream that fills it. My idea of how much ice cream I need expands to the size of the bowl I have. Time works in exactly the same way.

It's called Parkinson's Law, and it's the concept that "work expands so as to fill the time available for its completion." Let me translate this into regular English. This law states that if we give ourselves a week to complete a two-hour task, that task will increase in complexity and fill that week. While the two-hour task itself doesn't need the extra time, it's actually the stress and tension of having to get it done that fills the space.

Since the majority of that time is not necessary for the project itself, we can flip it on its head. If we do the opposite—if we *shorten* the time allowed for a task—we can use this law to our advantage to intensify our focus and make life easier . . . almost as easy as eating a bowl of ice cream. (Almost.)

Now we're not talking about magic here—if you give yourself a minute to complete a four-hour task, the task does not become so simple you can actually complete it in a minute. But you can try giving yourself half the time you think it would take to complete a task and see if you can actually complete it in that time.

The key to this mental trick is to treat this half-time deadline as a real and crucial deadline. Here's what life coach and author Marie Forleo had to say about this trick: "When you're up against a wall to complete a task, your genius gets focused like a laser beam."

Forleo shared an insightful example: Let's say you're making an introduction video for your website. You would probably give yourself a couple of weeks to complete it, right? Imagine, though, if Oprah called you and said, "Hey! We just had a cancellation and want to talk to you. In order to book you, though, my producers need to see your introduction video within the hour."

Would you give yourself weeks to make the short introduction video for Oprah? No, you'd bump it to the top of your list. I'm guessing you would clear your schedule to get on her show—you know, prioritize it. It would get done. We have the ability to do the work, but we often allow these tasks to drag out, stealing time from our day.

BUT WHAT WILL OTHERS THINK?

We get caught up in trying to do it all because we are trying to be perfect—to live the perfect life—to avoid the judgment of others. I think the hardest part about perfectionism is often the external pressure; there's so much perceived pressure from others to do things exactly right. We push ourselves to not make any mistakes because *perfectionism is rooted in the fear of failure.*

So we lean into our stories, our beliefs, making sure "we always" or "we never." We set impossibly high standards for ourselves, and when we don't reach those standards, we relentlessly criticize ourselves for failing.

We make light of it, though. We coyly say we're a bit of a perfectionist when asked about flaws in a job interview, or we laugh and say we just have a certain way we want things done—our way. But perfectionism in our lives can be debilitating.

Too often our work and our environment push us to this notion of "good perfectionism"—an oxymoron that is confused with striving for excellence or setting high personal standards (both of which are entirely different from perfectionism).

Perfectionism keeps us from being effective and pushes us to be efficient if for nothing more than appearances. Many experts believe that most people who suffer from perfectionistic tendencies are not born that way—in many cases we are trained by others' expectations and stories so that we take perfection onto ourselves to help protect us from failure. We don't realize that *without failure we wouldn't be as successful as we are.* Our shortcomings and mistakes are all part of our path.

The good news is, if perfectionism is more of a mindset, then we can adjust our expectations. We can begin to realize when we are in that headspace and redirect. We can adjust our way of thinking about what it means to be good enough. We can focus on what is truly important without the weight of others' judgment resting heavily on our shoulders.

Don't take others' burdens onto yourself. We seem to want to throw that weight on our backs, but doing so only slows our pace. We have to walk away from this idea of focusing on everyone else's happiness at the expense of our own. When we let go of the pressure of this Pinterest-crazed world, we allow ourselves the freedom to move forward onto the path our North Star is guiding us toward.

I cannot give you the gift of more time. If we allow ourselves to be honest, we know that even with more time we would continue packing our day full, like our overfilled bowl of ice cream, leaving us feeling bloated. We don't need to keep striving to do more; we need to prioritize the time we have so we can spend it on what matters most. That is what I want for us.

I know this might feel difficult—almost impossible—right now, but together we'll unpack a system to help in the next chapter.

LET ME HELP

I have a free download I'd love to share with you. It will help you track your time and begin to understand your unique ultradian rhythm. I'll guide you through the process with a video, making it even easier. You can get free access to this bonus feature at joyofmissingout.com/chapter5.

——— CHAPTER 6 ———

CLARIFY ENERGY

Instead of saying, "I don't have time," try saying,
"It's not a priority," and see how that feels.
LAURA VANDERKAM

We rush through our days, and more often than not we find ourselves with a to-do list that stretches about five miles long. We feel pride in that fat line crossing out a task, proving that we are qualified to wear our badge of busy.

But when all tasks are created equal, how does anyone know where to focus their energy? This is at the heart of why we spend our days running only to fall into bed at night wondering why it feels like nothing got done. It's because the important tasks—the tasks that should be at the top of our list—seem to fall to the side. The urgent tasks scream and cry out for our attention, so we spend our days putting out fires.

This is why you need to toss that to-do list straight into the fire. I know it's scary. As Marilyn Ferguson said, "It's Linus when his blanket is in the dryer. There's nothing to hold on to." You feel unstable because your brain craves those dopamine hits it gets every time you place a neat little check mark next to a task. But you gotta do it.

THE DARK SIDE OF THE TO-DO LIST

Our worth is not tied to the length of our to-do list. We allow this constrictive notion of merit to define us, but we are simply overwhelming ourselves. Remember our definition of what it means to be overwhelmed? *Overwhelm isn't having too much to do; it's not knowing where to start.* Our long checklist doesn't show us where to start. Instead, it confuses us more, spinning us in circles as we feverishly scan our tasks, wondering how we will possibly get it all done.

Yes, it makes us feel busy, but it doesn't make us productive—this is the dark side of the to-do list. It keeps us running all day long, never moving us closer to where we want to be. As Henry David Thoreau asked, "It's not enough to be busy; so are the ants. The question is, What are we busy about?" If we don't know, we're not really busy about anything—anything of importance to you, that is. It means we are wasting our precious energy in all the wrong places.

People love checking items off their to-do lists. Have you ever written down something on your list that you've already completed, just so you could check it off? I used to do that too. The problem is, if we are putting items on our lists *just to check them off,* then our lists aren't helping us be more effective—they are turning us into dopamine junkies.

Dopamine is a chemical in our brains that's responsible for the feeling of satisfaction we receive when we accomplish something. That good feeling you get when you cross an item off your list? Dopamine. Our brains love dopamine because it gives us that feel-good moment.

When we write down a list of tasks that are easy to cross off, we allow our brains to get addicted. We want that hit of dopamine, so without realizing it, we pack our lists full of menial tasks simply for the pleasure of crossing them off. We are using our lists as mood enhancers, not as productivity tools.

To-do lists tend to be unorganized and long because there's no filtering system. We simply add items as we think of them. When we scan our jumbled lists looking for our next task, our brains push us to choose the easiest wins—searching for a faster dopamine payoff. You see, dopamine doesn't distinguish between important and unimportant; it just knows that crossing items off our lists feels good. And that means that the important tasks on our lists end up waiting to get crossed off. Let's be honest, it's usually those longer tasks that will move us toward the life we want. Our true priorities continue to get pushed farther and farther down on our lists, forgotten and undone.

When we are focused mainly on short-term wins, we aren't making sure our day fits our bigger vision—our North Star visions of our lives. Instead, we end up spending large chunks of our time responding to fires simply because it feels so good to get that dopamine. This is why we feel busy. All. The. Time.

A survey of professionals conducted by LinkedIn found that by the end of the average workday, only 11 percent of professionals had accomplished all the tasks on their list. Our to-do lists are *supposed* to be a snapshot of our day, but here's the question: If 89 percent of professionals feel they've not accomplished their tasks, how do they feel at the end of the day?

To-do lists take energy away from the important tasks—the ones we must accomplish to create the impact we *really* want. We need to curate a list that highlights the route our North Star is guiding us toward, where each day we use our energy to get closer to our purpose and the big dreams and goals that go along with our North Star. We want a priority list. A priority list helps us look at the limited time we have so that we can choose where to spend our precious energy.

TO-DO LIST	PRIORITY LIST
LONG & UNATTAINABLE	SHORT & ACHIEVABLE
HAPHAZARD	FOCUSED ON CHOICES
UNORGANIZED	ORGANIZED
NO CLEAR DIRECTION	TELLS EXACTLY WHERE TO START

YOU NEED A PRIORITY LIST

When we use a priority list, we stop wasting energy deciding what to do next, or whether to start with the hardest or the easiest tasks—instead, we work by priority. Focusing on our priorities is what separates the busy from the truly productive.

A good priority list takes the same amount of time to create as a to-do list, but because you filter it through your priority levels, you consciously choose where to spend your energy—and where you don't. The list is structured for you to begin your day at the top with the highest priority tasks and work your way down. The feeling of overwhelm vanishes because you understand exactly where to start and what tasks you want to focus on next. You have a clear path for your day.

ESCALATE

CULTIVATE

ACCOMMODATE

Our priority list is made of three levels: Escalate, Cultivate, and Accommodate. Let's look at each one, starting with the top.

ESCALATE: IMPORTANT AND URGENT

These tasks are pushing us toward long-term goals *and* they have a pressing deadline.

FOCUSING ON OUR
PRIORITIES
IS WHAT
SEPARATES THE BUSY
—— FROM THE *truly* ——
PRODUCTIVE

EXAMPLES: last-minute adjustments to a project after receiving feed-back from your boss, your car breaking down, or a report or term paper with an imminent deadline.

This section goes at the top of our list because this is where we want to start our day. These items are our top priority—we need to escalate them. However, we don't want to spend *all* of our time on Escalated Tasks because, by being in urgency mode, we are playing beat-the-clock. If we focus *all* of our time on these Escalated Tasks, we don't allow ourselves the time to innovate or explore creative solutions. It's a defensive position, and we can't do our best work when we are in reactive mode.

We want to be effective and do our best work, so we want to avoid feeling this state of critical emergency and stress. We can actually eliminate many of our Escalated tasks by planning ahead. Long-term projects can be scheduled out so they're finished with plenty of time left (thus doing a better job *and* making them not urgent), the car can be taken in for regular maintenance so it does not break down, and so on.

We want to avoid Escalated situations whenever possible, but we'll never be able to eliminate them. Fires will always crop up—the boss assigns a last-minute presentation, the internet goes down, your kid gets sick at school—but for things that *are* in our control, we want to stay out of urgency mode.

CULTIVATE: IMPORTANT BUT NOT URGENT

These are activities that move us closer to our end goals because they are focused around future planning and self-improvement *but* have no looming deadline.

EXAMPLES: creating a budget plan, long-term projects, or developing processes and workflows.

Being in a situation without an urgent deadline allows us to do our best work because we have the time to really push ourselves and inno-vate. We can dive deeper into thinking of creative solutions; we are not in panic mode where we cannot think clearly. Because there's no urgency, though, we tend to push these items to the back burner until they finally do ignite, and then we end up feeling like we are fighting a wildfire with a garden hose.

While our priority list is divided into three sections, they are not evenly divided. *We need to place the most emphasis on this section.* This is the area where we will grow by leaps and bounds because we have time to nurture tasks and do our best work. We want to move out of urgency mode so we can be effective. The seeds we plant today we will cultivate, and they will grow fruit for the future.

ACCOMMODATE: UNIMPORTANT BUT URGENT

These are tasks with a pressing deadline, but they don't really help us focus on our North Star or our long-term goals.

EXAMPLES: the majority of the phone calls and emails we receive or volunteering for (or being pressured to accept) a project that does not align with our priorities. (This is the "good girl syndrome," when we just can't say no when someone asks us to do something.)

We want to spend as little time in this section as possible, but because of the urgency, these tasks tend to scream out louder than the rest.

I intentionally titled this priority level *Accommodate* to remind us that these tasks are less significant and shouldn't be at the top of our list. We simply need to accommodate them, not revolve our day around them. It's a mindset shift of bumping these screaming tasks to the bottom of the list, to be completed after we've done our important work. That may cause some discomfort, but we need some disruption in order to change what we've always done.

I would like to challenge you to think about what tasks you can get rid of completely in this section by either deleting or delegating them: Do you have to load the dishwasher yourself, or can the other members of the household do that? Do you have to pick up the phone every time you get a call in the middle of your work time, or can you set a boundary for when you have the time to devote to talking? This is where you need to comb through your tasks and figure out what you actually *do* want to spend your time doing or how you want to focus your energy.

I want to point out that unlike the Eisenhower Matrix, upon which this priority-list system is based, there's no fourth section of unimportant and nonurgent tasks. I intentionally designed this priority-list system to exclude those tasks. I don't think we should bother writing them down because they are not priorities in any way, shape, or form. They are best described as time wasters, so even the task of writing them out is precious time wasted.

Looking at our tasks by priority helps us see what needs to be done now (Escalate), what should be worked on for long-term wins (Cultivate), and what should be reevaluated (Accommodate). I know we keep going back to our definition of *overwhelm*, but it's true—when we know where to start, it empowers us to feel more in charge of ourselves and motivates us to work on the important areas of our life. A good priority list tells us exactly where to start.

Now that you understand the priority list, I want to pose a scenario for you to see where you would rank a task on your own list. Ready?

You bought a blue shirt at Target, only to get home and realize it just doesn't fit. The return deadline is in one week—where does this task fall on your list?

CIRCLE ONE: ESCALATE CULTIVATE ACCOMMODATE

Circled one? I'll check in at the end of this chapter and we'll see how you did.

URGENT VS. IMPORTANT

Prioritizing isn't hard, but one of the stumbling blocks I often see is that we confuse *urgent* with *important*. Many people think these words are synonymous and can be used almost interchangeably. Let's break them down:

IMPORTANT TASKS: contribute to our priorities; they fulfill what is at the heart of what we want to do; they are the stepping stones to move us toward our North Star.

URGENT TASKS: have a looming deadline; these are the tasks that are screaming at us, the fires that attract our attention.

At their core, *urgent tasks are tied only to time.* Because they are the items on your list with exclamation points, though, they tend to get your focus first—even if they are not tied to your priorities. In fact, most times they are not: the last-minute request from a coworker to help on a project she procrastinated on that has now hit its deadline, the pings on your phone from a friend who's got work drama, and probably 80 percent of what's in your email inbox at this very minute. We. Must. Check. Email.

Most of the urgent items on your list are not important; they just feel that way because they scream and yell. Urgent pushes and jostles its way in, elbowing out Important and bullying its way to the front, while Important sits undone. Here's a secret I want to share with you, though: *if you prioritize the important tasks, you get to a place where you don't have any urgent tasks.* You become proactive, and those fires don't even get a chance to ignite.

Urgency mode puts us in a reactive situation because we are working quickly against the clock. Importance mode puts us in a proactive position, allowing us to stay levelheaded and focused.

———

Jeanne was a student in my liveWELL Method course who was just weeks away from returning to work after maternity leave. She would meet on our live calls with her two adorable babies bouncing on her knee. She seemed to love her newfound motherhood and she loved her job, so she wanted to make sure she was giving work and home her true focus.

As any new mother will tell you, this is a challenge—there's so much to do, and adjusting to the new parenthood role takes some time.

I got some good insight into Jeanne's struggles when she shared one of her completed exercises with me. The lesson was focused on looking at a list of tasks and deciding what on the list is important and what is merely urgent. [Spoiler alert: Most of the tasks on this list (and your list) are urgent but not important.]

Jeanne, though, had listed every single item as important. Every single one. No wonder she felt overwhelmed. Caring for two new babies is hard enough, but when you don't know your top priority, it's extraordinarily difficult to know where to start—which is when overwhelm sets in. I don't think Jeanne is alone, though. We rush through our days putting out so many fires that we don't have time to stop and ask ourselves what needs to happen first.

GETTING CLEAR ON WHAT'S IMPORTANT

Not understanding what is important causes us to have priority blindness. Similar to the information blindness I talked about in chapter 3, we are so bombarded with tasks and requests that they blind us and we lose sight of what is truly important.

And so we continue to pile more and more priorities on ourselves, which does nothing but weigh us down, keeping us from the life we want. We have to ask ourselves: Weighed down as we are, what do we throw overboard when our boat is sinking?

There's nothing like an emergency to crystallize what's important. When your ship is sinking, it suddenly becomes easy to decide what to jettison over the side—certainly not the family heirlooms or photo albums. In moments like these, it's easier to realize that everything else is just dead-weight dragging your boat down into the murky depths.

You don't want to wait for a crisis to help you gain clarity on what's important. You don't need to wait until your boat is floundering to decide where to spend your energy. You need to become CLEAR on what is most important.

Important tasks are hard to define, I know. To make the process easier, I've created the CLEAR framework to help you differentiate the important from the merely urgent:

C ONNECTED TO YOUR NORTH STAR
L INKED TO A GOAL
E SSENTIAL
A DVANTAGEOUS
R EALITY-BASED

The process of "getting CLEAR" is easy, and you can do it anywhere—just use what I call the five-finger test. Ask yourself the five questions in the CLEAR framework, and each time you answer yes, simply raise a finger. If you have three or more fingers raised, you know the item deserves to be treated as important. Two fingers or fewer? That's an unimportant task.

ASK YOURSELF: IS THIS CONNECTED TO MY NORTH STAR?

I talked in the first section of the book about the importance of a North Star and how we use it to help us intentionally make choices. Your North Star determines how you want to spend your time, energy, and focus—the three key commodities when it comes to productivity. It can also help clarify what's important.

Herb Kelleher, former CEO of Southwest Airlines, is a great example of a person who had to make big decisions all day every day. When he was CEO, he filtered his decision making process by asking this question: Will this help Southwest be the low-cost provider?

Southwest's mission was to "connect people to what's important in their lives through friendly, reliable, and low-cost air travel," so you can see that Kelleher's filtering question is tied directly to that North Star. Using this filter paid off; Southwest Airlines has continually been an award-winning airline and has found success even in tough economic times while other airlines have failed.

Questions to Go Deeper:

- Is this tied to my mission statement?

- Does this task align with my core values?
- Is this going to help me move closer to my vision?

ASK YOURSELF: IS IT LINKED TO A GOAL?

*I always knew I'd be a millionaire by age thirty-two. In fact, I
am going to be the richest black woman in America.*
OPRAH WINFREY, 1986

It took Oprah years to accomplish her goal, but I think we can all agree
she crushed it. She didn't have a magic ball; instead, she had been setting
goals her entire career.

As she puts it, "The big secret in life is that there is no big secret.
Whatever your goal, you can get there if you're willing to work." That
work becomes easier if we consistently, intentionally work toward our larger
goals. When we set goals, we direct our energy in a forward motion. Our
goals drive us closer to the ideal life we are seeking.

Earlier in the chapter I talked about the ineffective tendency to choose
tasks we can easily tick off our list. Really, though, we should be spending
our energy on the deeper work. If you can link the needle-moving tasks to
your goals, it transforms them into a meaningful decision. As I discussed
in chapter 4, goals are an extension of the foundation we create with our
North Star.

Because they help us get to the vision we have for ourselves, goals
should be a key part of our decision-making process when deciding if a task
is important. When we link our daily tasks to our goals, we make small
steps forward every single day. Small steps lead to bigger steps, which then
lead to running. That's the momentum we need.

Questions to Go Deeper:
- Is this task a key part of accomplishing my goal?
- Is this chore propelling me closer to my goal?

ASK YOURSELF: IS IT ESSENTIAL?

*I don't read work emails after 7 p.m. or on weekends. And if
you work for me, may I suggest you put down your phone.*

This is Shonda Rhimes's email signature, which makes it evident that
even one of the most successful producers in Hollywood is a woman with
well-defined boundaries. You need boundaries too.

Whether you are CEO of the office or the home (or both!), *you have
to keep in mind that CEO doesn't stand for Chief Everything Officer.* Ask
yourself: *What are the obligations I am taking on that could be done by
someone else?*

Rhimes views delegation as opportunities for growth. To create a multitude of successful shows, she needs to allow others to rise and take on
tasks. "I look at it this way," she shared. "If the thing that ABC is paying
me for is storytelling—not to make sure that a costume is exactly right or
all those other things—then it is up to me . . . so that that function of my
job can happen."

She admits that if you allow it, work will fill all your time 24 hours a
day, 365 days a year. Parkinson's law applies to all of us regardless of fame
or fortune. As Rhimes said, "It suddenly occurred to me that unless I just
say, 'That's not going to happen,' it was always going to happen."

Questions to Go Deeper:
- Is this something that needs to be done by me?
- Is this something I cannot outsource or delegate?

ASK YOURSELF: IS IT ADVANTAGEOUS?

We want to consistently work on tasks that have a return on investment—
the time we put into them pays off in dividends down the road. Our time is
a finite commodity that we are consistently investing in the tasks and chores
we choose to do, so you need to question how you are spending this time.

Remember the Pareto Principle that I discussed in chapter 5? I shared that Warren Buffett attributes 90 percent of his wealth to just ten of the companies he had invested in. Where do you think he spends his energy?

Buffett shared, "The difference between successful people and really successful people is that really successful people say no to almost everything." While he used to pursue shiny objects, he realized chasing after every idea only wore him out. He uses a two-list strategy to help him zero in on his 20 percent. Buffett says to write down twenty-five goals or tasks, then circle the top five. Those are your focus.

And what do you do with the other twenty? Forget about them. According to Buffett, they're only distractions until you've achieved success with your top five. Remember, focused energy creates the biggest impact.

Keep in mind, however, that there's more to life than goals. *I know— can you believe I just said that?* But there is. To live a wholistic* life, you need to make sure you are continuing to spend some amount of time on tasks that are connected to a cause, a belief—something that impassions you. These tasks may not be directly tied to your goals or your North Star, but they are deeply satisfying. *Do not undervalue work that feeds your soul.*

Questions to Go Deeper:

- Is this allowing me to focus on the key parts of my business or life that will help me grow?
- Is this fulfilling to me spiritually, emotionally, or psychologically?

ASK YOURSELF: IS IT REALITY-BASED?

Oftentimes we feel that something is important because we believe it's something we are supposed to do—even if it's not something we really want. These tasks are so deeply entwined with our stories and our need for perfection that we don't even realize it. We feel tied to the obligation, and we lose sight of why we are even doing the task in the first place.

---

* I use *wholistic* because it represents the whole self.

I think one of the best ways to illustrate this is by sharing how my own stories led me to misunderstand what's important.

For years I told myself a story: a good mom always bakes birthday cakes for her family. I don't know where this belief came from, but it was definitely one of the requirements, in my head, to be the perfect mom.

I baked lemon cakes for John, strawberry cakes for Kate, and chocolate cakes for Jack. I normally enjoy baking the cakes, even if they aren't beautifully decorated like the ones in the pastry shop window. One fall, though, baking felt more like a task than a treat. I was fresh off the fall launch of our planners, was prepping for the launch on my course, and had several speaking events. The thought of baking a cake from scratch about did me in. I was going to do it, though, no matter what. I *had* to make that cake; I was determined to be a good mom.

About four days before Kate's birthday, we went out to pick up my baking supplies. I was stressed. And tired. And unmotivated. But I plastered a smile on my face and herded us out the door—I was doing this!

As we went into the grocery store, I noticed Kate peering at the bakery case.

"Would you like me to buy you a cake?" I teased, laughing at the idea.

She looked up with a hint of longing. "Could we?"

I stopped short. "Really?" I asked.

"Oh yes!" she said excitedly. *Really?!* I thought to myself. And then she timidly asked, "Could they write my name on it? In cursive? With flowers?"

Why yes, my love, they could.

At that moment I realized I was prioritizing all wrong. I was thinking all about *my* expectations—not hers. Together we picked out a cake, and my girl was so pleased I could hardly stand it. All that stress. All that fretting—because I hadn't thought to ask what she really wanted. I decided in that moment that the following year I'd happily make her a cake from scratch or buy one from the store. Really, it's up to her.

Let's ask ourselves: Are we allowing our stories to dictate our days?

Questions to Go Deeper:

- Is this task something that really needs to happen or is it tied to a story I am telling myself?
- Am I getting caught up in perfectionism and nit-picking this in an effort to make it perfect?

THE BLUE SHIRT REVISITED

Remember that shirt you bought at Target? Did you decide which priority level it should be assigned?

Usually when I share this scenario, people say it's an Escalated Task. When I ask why, they say it's urgent because it needs to be returned soon. And I agree, it is an urgent task.

But is it important? Generally someone will tell me they want their money back or they need to be mindful of their budget; therefore, it's important. But is it? Using the CLEAR framework, is this task *really* important?

It actually fits under the section of our list labeled *Accommodate*—urgent but unimportant. I want to clarify that just because something is at the bottom of the list doesn't mean it doesn't get done—it just gets done last. After we complete our important work, then we tackle the unimportant. Don't *start* your day running to Target—*end* your day there. We aren't throwing out our tasks in the Accommodate level of our list; we just are not focusing the majority of our prime time on them.

I shared this T-shirt story as part of a keynote I was giving to CEOs not that long ago. Hannah, a powerhouse CEO from Silicon Valley, approached me afterward and challenged this idea. She agreed with me that the task should be labeled *Accommodate*, but she informed me that her time was not worth the return trip to Target. She explained that she pays herself a virtual hourly rate of $5,000, and to spend thirty minutes was not a good use of her time. She said, "I would donate it. Give it to someone who needs it."

As you can imagine, I liked Hannah immediately. She's right. Even if you don't virtually pay yourself $5,000 an hour, you will spend $5 on gas to return a $15 shirt. Not to mention the time you will spend driving across town, standing in line, and somehow ending up spending yet another $100 at Target (*you know we all do it*).

Take that time and money and spend it somewhere you *do* deem important. If sticking to your budget is high on your list of priorities, take five minutes to try on the shirt before you leave the store. That's a five-minute investment to make sure you don't waste thirty later on.

TO-DO LIST   PRIORITY LIST

In the busy throes of everyday life, we all have moments when we lose sight of our priorities. It's easy to push what's important aside to make room for the loud and obnoxious urgent that's pulling us in all directions.

Your decisions set the course for your destination. In section 1, we set the path for our North Star, and now we have the clarity to begin our journey. In moments when you find yourself turning in circles, just as I did in my kitchen all those years ago, stop and take a deep breath and ask yourself the five CLEAR questions:

> *Is it **C**onnected to my North Star?*
> *Is it **L**inked to a goal?*
> *Is it **E**ssential?*
> *It is **A**dvantageous?*
> *Is it **R**eality-based?*

Then put the task where it belongs on your priority list. Starting from the top and working your way down that list will give you the clarity you need to know how to spend your time, energy, and focus in ways that move you forward toward your ideal life.

CREATE SIMPLICITY

3   *Simplify productivity systems customized to you to help life run smoothly and with less effort.*

So many productivity books focus on how we can work better in our office space but forget the importance of productivity at home. It does us no good to bring home the bacon and fry it up in a pan if the kitchen is burning down around us. Without a strong and stable home life, we cannot excel at work. This is part of the wholistic approach to productivity that makes the liveWELL Method unique—it's not just about being effective at work but making sure life is running smoothly at home as well.

In the third step of the liveWELL Method, we will work together to create healthy habits that will focus your time and energy on what you really want to achieve. We will design effective routines and systems to make sure you are carving out time for you and your priorities. We will "take the thinking out of it" so your life can run more smoothly and easily, allowing you to spend more of your time on what's truly important.

CHAPTER 7

SIMPLIFY SYSTEMS

What I do every day matters more than
what I do once in a while.
GRETCHEN RUBIN

I'm a terrible runner. Sometimes I see people running along the road, blissfully moving like graceful antelopes, and I so desperately want that. I imagine myself running *Chariots of Fire*–style with the slow piano playing in the background. I go and lace up my shoes, I spend fifteen minutes stretching and I run like an antelope. Until ten minutes later—when I remember how much I truly don't like running. I'm red-faced, out of breath, and officially out. Spent. No gas left in the tank and no real desire to keep running.

You see, I'm in love with the *idea* of running—not the running itself.

And I believe that's how people feel when they see these highly disciplined ways of living. We see an image on Pinterest of a pantry where the food is divided into twenty-five thousand labeled containers (which are, of course, color coordinated!), or we read a book telling us that we need to fold our clothes in a very strict, very precise way, and we think, *Yes! This—this is what I need!*

We gather all the supplies, and we fold our clothes military style for fifteen minutes—until reality sets in. And then we are spent. No gas left in the tank and no real desire to use a ten-step process to fold a shirt.

Yes, the images are Pinterest-worthy, but is that really the life you want to live? I'll be honest, being a highly disciplined person sounds terrible—all that time *not* doing what you really want to do? You are setting yourself up for a future with some serious marble jar moments.

That's for the birds, my friend. Because here's the truth: it's not discipline you need—it's simple systems. Good, healthy systems aligned with the priorities we discovered in section 1 of this book. And the best news? Good systems run on autopilot once we establish them.

Systems are a key part of living the life we want, because while it's important to spend time focused on priorities, we still have all the other tasks to do. There are the not-so-glamorous activities like home maintenance, managing finances, getting dinner on the table, and then there's laundry.

What is it about laundry? It seems to be the bane of everyone's existence. How is it possible that we need a mountain's worth of clothes cleaned every single week? But we do. All these things must be done.

How do we keep everything running and still make time for what's important? I hear women asking, begging to know if there's a magic solution—and there is. Systems. Strong systems harness the patterns of habits and make tasks happen automatically. Like I said—magic.

When I typed that paragraph, I literally felt myself exhale, because that's how I feel when I have systems in place. Systems make our lives easier. Doesn't that sound like something we all want? But we have a tendency to overcomplicate tasks when really we just need to break them down into bite-size pieces that feel manageable and achievable.

EAT THAT ELEPHANT

Have you heard the phrase "eat the elephant"? It comes from the African proverb, "The best way to eat an elephant standing in your path is to cut it up into little pieces." Now I'm not serving elephant for dinner at my house, but I do have a mountain of laundry in my path (which could be mistaken for an elephant) and about a thousand other things that must be done.

This concept of taking a big item and breaking it down into pieces applies to our tasks, projects, goals—basically anything we want to tackle. *Bite-size wins build momentum* and bring us a little satisfaction bit by bit. Happiness increases if we view our tasks as a series of many small milestones instead of one huge, looming chore. While laundry isn't scary, it is overwhelming to think we will never get it accomplished, which is why we put it off or why we feel so irritated by it. Small bites, though, give us something achievable to focus on.

Let's go back to my ten minutes of antelope-like glory. (It's a short-lived phenomenon, so I need to stretch it out where I can.) I don't ever think about running a mile because if I did I would never even lace up my shoes. Running, for me, is an elephant.

I think about what's doable for me. *All right,* I think to myself, *I can make it to the stop sign* (which, mind you, is about 150 yards away). When I make it to the sign, I get a little sense of accomplishment and I'm encouraged to keep moving. *Next up, the blue car. Then the brick house . . . and then the fire hydrant.* My feet move one in front of the other until that entire elephant is stuffed down my throat, bite by bite.

MAKE IT WORK FOR YOU

Here's the catch, though: systems need to work for you. They should be tightly bound to the life we *really* want to live; they should play to our strengths and our weaknesses to make life feel easier.

We flip through magazines, we scroll through social media, and we see these beautiful images of meticulously organized kitchens, exquisitely decorated office spaces, and elaborate homemade meals. We think that's the life we are supposed to have, and we feel inadequate because our lives are not magazine-worthy.

We lose time DREAMING *of a* LIFE WE COULD HAVE WHEN THE ONE RIGHT IN FRONT OF US COULD BE *even more* beautiful

You need to ask yourself:

Are you looking for a Pinterest-worthy life, or are you craving the life that feels happy to you?
Do you want a Facebook-worthy life where you worry whether the napkins are pressed and if you should make homemade chocolate chips?
Are you searching for an Instagram-worthy life where you stress about if the pillows on the couch are at the right angle or if your abs look good in a bikini top you would never wear in public anyway?

I'm guessing, though, that you are more like me. I've got enough on my plate worrying about whether I'm raising responsible kids, whether I'm accomplishing my goals, and whether my work feels strong.

We lose time dreaming of a life we *could* have, when the one right in front of us could be even more beautiful and livable. We need to create systems that feel attainable and fit the lifestyle we really want—not the one we think we are *supposed* to want.

When I was growing up, we always had a set of color-coordinated towels in every size imaginable perfectly placed on the towel bar in each bathroom. I remember asking my mother why. *Why did we have such fancy, fluffy towels in our bathrooms that no one was allowed to use?* I found it baffling; it made no sense.

I recall her shrugging her shoulders as she meticulously refolded and straightened the towels on the bar and explained, "We have these towels because that's just what you are supposed to do."

That's what we are supposed to do.

Our job isn't to question why; it's to live up to the expectations.

It wasn't her fault. She was following the rules—the story she told herself: *ladies with nice houses have beautifully useless linens for no one to use.* Ever.

I think that's the moment I decided I would never have a towel bar in my bathroom. And I don't. Every time I move into a house, I take down the towel bars and put in a set of hooks. In my heart of hearts, I'm honest with myself. I know I won't trifold a towel and position it beautifully on the bar. Quite frankly, no one else in my house will either. But we will place it on a hook.

Keeping the bathroom clean can be an elephant, but there are no dirty towels on my floor because I didn't fight against my weaknesses. Instead, I acknowledged them and built a system to work for me. It's the same with clothes. I am not good at folding clothes and I don't enjoy it. There are about ten thousand things I'd rather do than fold clothes, including hanging by my fingernails.

Recognizing my weakness, I set up closets so more clothes can be hung. Very few items go into drawers, and those that do have bins to create sections that allow me to toss in items like socks and underwear while keeping everything organized. I don't want to spend my life folding. I want to spend it living.

Systems should bring harmony to your life, but when they aren't in tune they can feel disruptive. Rigid systems with no flexibility are primed to fail because they are made of glass—marble jar glass.

Systems need to work for you. Play to your strengths *and* your weaknesses. Let's embrace our imperfectly beautiful selves and then make our systems work to our advantage. This might be why we've all started and quit a thousand different ways to keep ourselves organized, resulting in us feeling like failures. But it was the system that failed—not us. The system simply didn't work for the way *we* work.

Designing our systems to work with our strengths and *weaknesses sets us up for success.* This is true because when we fight against our natural tendencies and inclinations, we wear ourselves out.

TAKE THE THINKING OUT OF IT

Your brain takes up a mere 2 percent of your body mass but consumes an astonishing 20 percent of your calories each day. Your brain is a calorie-burning machine, so it loves to conserve energy when it can. Then it can apply big effort to the important items you want to tackle, like your goals.

Your brain, just like your body, has a limited amount of calories, and when your brain is working hard making decisions, it wears itself out. Decision fatigue sets in.

That moment at the end of the day when you feel brain-dead? That feeling is real—your brain is literally running out of calories and just can't function. It's not about willpower or discipline. Your brain simply has no gas left in the tank and no real desire to keep making good choices.

Most times we aren't even aware we are low on mental energy, and our brain continues working but starts to look for shortcuts. It does this in two different ways:

ACTS IMPULSIVELY: In other words, it stops spending the energy needed to think through your actions.

> *I'm hungry and the donut that's been sitting out in the break room since yesterday looks good. I should eat it.*

DOES NOTHING: We simply choose not to choose.

> *I know my budget is tight, but I can't decide which of these pairs of shoes looks better. I'll get both.*

Our perfectly rational brain loses its ability to make good decisions when we overload it with work. In a Stanford University study, researchers divided students into two groups. Group A had to memorize a two-digit number while Group B memorized a seven-digit number. After memorizing the number, they were asked to walk down a hall where they were offered two snack choices: a piece of cake or fruit salad. Students who memorized the seven digits were twice as likely to choose the unhealthy snack as Group A.

When we give the brain extra work—in this case, simply five extra numbers to memorize—it gets overloaded and loses its ability to make good decisions. Knowing the right choice takes brainpower, and when we overtax our brains with extra thinking, we use up this valuable resource.

———

Understanding decision fatigue felt like a lightbulb moment for Holly. As a former army officer, she was used to making fast-paced, often life-altering, decisions in her job. Being retired means that many of her decisions may seem less significant, but in her own words, "Since they involve my family, they are at the top of my 'Get it right the first time' list. . . . I don't want to keep space in my mind for 'What do I have to do next?' Let's just write it down and make it a scheduled item. Less stress, less worry—I know I've got it handled."

There's a lot of empowerment in that last statement of Holly's—it feels good, doesn't it? When we feel like we have it handled—like we can count our marbles instead of smashing those jars? Confidence looks good on Holly. It looks good on you too.

Holly is taking charge and taking the thinking out of it. That's what we need to do too. When we spend our days uncertain where to focus, burning through the calories in our brains, our brainpower depletes and we can no longer use it on important tasks. We want to get our brains working at full capacity by allowing them to focus on what's most important—not on trivial decisions that need to be made.

Using habits to our advantage does that. Tying habits into our systems allows us to streamline our thinking and helps eliminate decision fatigue so we can spend our energy in the most impactful way.

GOOD HABITS GET A BAD RAP

Habit can feel like a bad word. We hear about habits and we think about biting our nails or snacking too much or smoking. We think all habits are bad, but researchers at Duke University actually found that about 40 to 45 percent of the actions we make each day are actually habits, not really decisions.

Think about it. How taxing would it be if we had to think about every little action we make throughout our day? What would it be like if we had to concentrate every morning on getting dressed? When we first learned to put on our pants as toddlers, it took immense effort. We had to sit down on the floor, legs splayed out in front of us, as we put in one leg, then the other. With tongues poking out between our lips (somehow helping us focus our attention), we wrestled with getting the pants hiked up and untwisted.

And don't get me started on that button at the top! I vividly remember my mom buying me my first pair of button fly jeans and thinking that woman was crazy to think I would ever get it figured out and buttoned in less than ten minutes!

The good news is that I did eventually master my button fly, and I'm guessing you did too. We now get dressed without giving it a second thought—we can have a conversation or watch TV while doing it. Here's what's really interesting: you probably don't realize this, but each time you put on your pants, you put the same leg in first. Yes, every time. You see, putting on pants is a habit.

Using habits allows your brain to focus its energy on what really matters in your day. Charles Duhigg, author of *The Power of Habit*, shared that when you start implementing habits, "the brain starts working less and less. The brain can almost completely shut down. . . . And this is a real advantage, because it means you have all of this mental activity you can devote to something else." Something else, you know, like your priorities and goals. Habits free up our mental space so we can focus.

People who appear to be disciplined are really people who have harnessed the power of habits. This is what makes them seem disciplined when in reality a never-ending supply of willpower doesn't exist.

We need to leverage our habits to free up our brain space, to take the thinking out of it and allow ourselves the ability to make the choices that really matter. Building strong habits isn't hard; it just takes some extra energy at the beginning. Once they are established, habits require less effort, less energy, and less thinking to maintain. They take the thinking out of tasks. Your brain stops wasting calories and channels all its energy to move you forward.

THE FOUR STEPS TO CREATING HABITS

1 | **ARTICULATE**
THE HABIT

4 | **MAKE**
A PLAN

HABITS

2 | **IDENTIFY**
THE CUES

3 | **DEFINE**
THE BEHAVIOR

ARTICULATE THE HABIT

The first step is to articulate the habit. Ask yourself, *Why do I want to build a new habit?* Anytime we want to start something new, we should begin with a foundation of why. We want to allow our North Star to be our constant guide, making the choice clear. This, of course, speaks directly to our internal locus of control we talked about in chapter 2 and helps increase our motivation to cultivate this habit.

IDENTIFY THE CUES

Next, we need to identify the cues. Duhigg defines these as the trigger to tell our brain to instigate the habit. He believes there are five cues: location, time, emotional state, other people, and preceding action. Cues can be as simple as leaving our gym shoes by the door to help trigger us to run after work or leaving our planners on our desks to remind us to start each day by creating a priority list. Cues are the biggest key to unlocking our habits because once we know what triggers an action, we can begin to define our behavior.

DEFINE THE BEHAVIOR

What actions do we want to make into a healthy habit? An important part of defining the behavior is understanding what habits expert Gretchen

Rubin calls "loopholes." She wrote, "When we try to form and keep habits, we often search . . . for justifications that will excuse us from keeping this particular habit." We need to identify our potential stumbling blocks—ahem, excuses we'll use—so we can set ourselves up for success.

Setting and establishing habits takes effort at the beginning. It might be tempting to think of this as one more thing on your plate, but this is an investment.

In my liveWELL Method course, Brenda shared she was bristling against this idea at first. She said, "I have felt for a while that life was controlling me, instead of the other way around, so I've been trying to reclaim it." You may have felt this way yourself. Trust me, you are not alone in feeling like your plate is already too full.

This idea of adding structure might feel unappealing because in our hearts we want to "run and be free," like Brenda said. I hear you. At the beginning, it does take effort because it requires conscious work to create these habits. But give it some time. Most people have a sweet spot of about sixty-six days for a habit to set.

Once a habit sticks, it should feel *less constraining* because you effectively take the thinking out of the action long term. Forming a habit does take intention, so it's important to make sure not to skip the final step—make a plan.

MAKE A PLAN

A good plan includes the three Rs—*record*, *reward*, and *redirect*. We want to track our progress. When we are working on cultivating daily habits, it's difficult for us to see our progress unless we find a way to track growth. *What gets written gets measured; what gets measured gets achieved.* Progress is a bit like watching our children grow: we simply cannot see it until one day they are suddenly towering over us. We want to be mindful with establishing these habits, so it's important to stop and take note. A simple habit tracker is ideal in helping you track and measure your progress.

Another important part of creating a plan is to make sure you reward yourself. Small rewards work as celebrations and springboards to keep you moving. The reward can be as small as giving yourself a kind word or listening to a favorite song.

Brain research shows that rewards are a key part of setting the patterns of habits in place. Once the habit becomes set, the reward is no longer needed, but we require positive reinforcement at the beginning to act as a message to the brain, telling it this is an activity worth remembering in the future. Remember, the reward is not the end goal. It's just a way to push you forward and encourage your brain to accept the habit.

Let me share some unfiltered honesty with you—we will stumble. We will stray off track—it happens to all of us. We need to remind ourselves that habits take time and there may be days when we forget our cues or feel frustrated. We can't get caught up when we fail; we need to be prepared to pick ourselves back up, recover, and redirect.

Take time and allow the process to unfold, because it is worth it. Over time, this loop becomes one solidifying action—a habit that essentially takes the thinking out of a task. Your brain stops wasting calories and instead channels all its energy to move you forward. Habits are only difficult at the beginning; then they become easy because they require less effort, less energy, and less thinking to maintain once they are established.

The trick is just understanding and unlocking our habits so we can cultivate the healthy ones and curb the ones we don't really like.

BREAKING BAD HABITS

I've walked with you through the process of establishing a habit—but what about habits we don't really love? What about the ones we want to break? Let me share how I used this same process to my own advantage to break a bad habit and then establish a new, healthier one.

I am terrible about checking email. Terrible in the sense that I'm like Pavlov's dog. Every time I hear the little ping of a new email, I must immediately stop what I'm doing and go check it. I don't have this issue with texts or phone calls—just email. The need for the little hit of dopamine mixed with my perfectionism addiction drives me to constantly strive to zero out my inbox count.

If I am in the middle of deep work, if I'm in the midst of reading a book with my kids, or even if I am having a conversation, when I hear that ping I begin to feel the itch. It's like a scratchy tag on the back of my shirt, irritating me, calling to me to stop whatever I'm doing to go check it. It doesn't seem to matter that at least 25 percent of the time it's spam. In my mind, it must be checked immediately.

My first step was acknowledging this weakness. I had to admit I somehow accidentally built up a habit of checking email incessantly and I needed to stop. I knew I wanted to limit my email time so I could reclaim my time for my important work—that was my *why*.

I channeled my inner Nancy Drew and discovered I had a few cues that caused me to be in my inbox far too much: the ping of the computer when a new email arrived (preceding action) and the inbox email count at the bottom of my screen clearly mocking me (emotional state). These two cues were like a siren song calling me into the depth of my inbox and out of the space where I truly wanted to be. I needed to kill the cues and redefine my behavior. I set a goal to establish a new habit of checking email four times a day: in the morning, before lunch, midafternoon, and early evening. I set a reminder on my phone to notify me when it was time to dive into my inbox.

I'll be honest: thinking of checking only four times a day almost gave me the shakes because I have a couple of excuses I tell myself. Gretchen Rubin would define these loopholes as "concern for others" (*Other people rely on me to reply quickly!*) and "lack of control" (*I can't help myself!*). I acknowledged that these were excuses and set myself up for success.

Then I made my plan. Other than my four check-in times, my email program would have to be closed out to eliminate the temptation, and any noisy notifications were turned off on my phone. No blips, no pips, no beeps from email. I even turned off the vibrate option. I was serious.

I figured I was spending at least an extra thirty minutes of my day mindlessly checking email, so to reward myself, I gifted those thirty minutes back. I set myself up with a habit tracker to keep up with my progress, and on the days I did well, I used my thirty bonus minutes to do whatever I wanted. I read chapters in fiction books, I took baths, I painted my nails—all things I told myself I didn't have time to do before. It took time, but I now feel more in control of my email—it no longer controls me. And that's a good feeling.

That's the feeling I want to permeate our days. With systems in place we have less stress, we are more effective, and nothing falls through the cracks. We have to let go, however, of the unattainable and the unrealistic. When we create systems playing to our strengths and weaknesses, we have gas in our tanks and real desire for the life we are living.

Let's stop worrying about running like an antelope—trying to be what we are not. Turn off the *Chariots of Fire* music and put on your own soundtrack, the one that fits you and your life. Let's work together to build simple systems for you to make life feel easier, run more smoothly, and maybe bring you a glass of wine at the end of the day.*

---

* Okay, full disclosure, no system will bring you wine . . . but it can give you the time to sit down at the end of the day and enjoy a little victory lap.

CHAPTER 8

SIMPLIFY ROUTINES

The decisions you make determine the schedule you keep.
The schedule you keep determines the life you live. And how
you live your life determines how you spend your soul.
LYSA TERKEURST

I have a beautiful blue-green platter I pull out of my cabinet every year on Christmas Eve. It's exactly the right size for the crab I've roasted in butter and spices. The table is covered with a large sheet of craft paper, and I know exactly what dishes I'll use for the Caesar salad and homemade bread. The peppermint ice cream I made earlier in the day is sitting in the freezer, ready to be pulled out after we put on our freshly unwrapped new pajamas. We'll eat ice cream and play games through the night until it's time to head to our rooms to dream of sugarplums. That's what we do every year—my entire family starts anticipating it almost as soon as the Halloween decorations come down. It's our tradition.

I love traditions. I love how they weave together years' and years' worth of family time. I believe the big memories and feelings we have from our childhood are really a series of these traditions stitched together over time, creating a solid memory. After I became a mother, I was *so* conscious of

117

this with my children. I created all these little traditions we use to celebrate each passing year. And now that my children are older, I believe even more strongly that these traditions have pulled us closer together as a family.

The side bonus of these traditions is the extra boost they give to your productivity. You see, traditions are one of the very best ways to take the extra stress and work out of those busy times. Let me tell you what I mean—the holiday dinner I told you about seems like a whole lotta work, but it's all so easy because it's a tradition. I don't have to worry about what's for dinner—all the recipes are already pulled together in a binder along with notes I've written to myself over the years on when I need to pop each thing into the oven or what I can make ahead of time.

I don't worry about what activity we'll do—I know we'll each unwrap brand-new pajamas along with one present with a new game inside. I don't even have to worry about what I'll wear! Traditions allow me to make time special for my family, but they also make it so much easier for me to sit back and actually enjoy the time instead of rushing around stressing. You see, traditions are systems—they take the thinking out of tasks. Routines and rituals do that for us, too, but on a daily basis—they help streamline our days and make it easier for us to enjoy each day.

 Sidebar with me here for just a second: yes, I go a little bananas with the cooking, but that's because I love to cook. On holidays it's like I get the chance to pretend I'm a big-time chef with my own cooking show—it's something fulfilling for me. I will tell you this: I don't do holiday cards, I don't go crazy with holiday decorating, and if there was an award for Worst Elf-on-a-Shelf Mom, I'd be holding that prize. You do you. Do the traditions you love.

ROUTINES DON'T HAVE TO FEEL ROUTINE

We all look forward to our traditions, don't we? Whether it's birthday traditions, holiday traditions, or even Sunday morning pancake traditions, the anticipation of them is almost as enjoyable as the actions themselves. Traditions have a way of making events seem special, of marking time with intention. We don't have to wait for special events to make rituals for ourselves. We can have routines to make each day feel special and allow the room we need for the tasks we really want to do each day.

Routines are essentially habits following one after the other, each one acting as a cue for the next, building momentum. And momentum is what we need. Sometimes it's the things that appear to be really small that effect the greatest change—this is called the domino effect.

We've all played with dominoes at some point in our lives, lining them up in intricate patterns simply for the thrill of watching them knock one another down. But in 1983 physicist Lorne Whitehead discovered that while dominoes can knock down lots of other dominoes, they can also topple dominoes 50 percent larger than themselves.

Let's think about this a second. This means a single, tiny domino alone can't knock down a one-thousand-foot-tall domino, *but* if we start with one tiny domino and line up sixteen more—each 50 percent larger than the last—it could. Domino number seventeen, while taller than the Empire State Building, would topple over, brought down by a force started by a two-inch domino.

To make big changes happen, we simply need to start small and allow the dominoes to fall. Little steps lead to giant leaps toward the life we want to live. Every day we need to line up our priorities, find our lead domino, and push it over to make the next big thing happen. *Small wins lead to big victories.*

Instead of dominoes, though, let's use our routines. Let's create a process where we line up our habits in a logical order to help us build this momentum. The idea is to complete a number of things without even thinking about it—each domino knocking down the next.

In some ways, you probably already do this. Think about your morning: you get up, brush your teeth, shower, put on deodorant, and so on. How often do you have to think actively about each of these steps? The reality is, you probably don't—you've created a routine for yourself. So why not design a routine with intention? A routine that allows the space you want for what matters most.

Let me explain what I mean. While working on this book, I needed to carve out space to write. I knew that if I tried to shoehorn in writing time where my day allowed, this book would take me decades to finish. I decided to prioritize this book, so I made a commitment to design a morning routine that allowed writing to be a focus.

Each morning my alarm goes off around 4:30 a.m. Yes, for a night owl like me, that's early! But this book is important, so this is a gift of time I'm giving to this priority right now. I lie in bed for ten minutes because this is my time to center myself; I use it to pray and meditate. At 4:40 I crawl quietly from the bed so I don't wake up John, and sneak into the bathroom to brush my teeth, wash my face, and gulp down a sixteen-ounce glass of water.

My morning water was one of the first habits I worked hard to instill in my routine. I was waking up groggy and cranky, but I learned that these symptoms are often caused by dehydration. Our bodies are made up of almost 60 percent water, and when we sleep we are going almost eight hours without hydration, making our brains sluggish.

I used my teeth brushing as a springboard to build this habit. As my cue, I placed an empty glass in front of my sink where I couldn't possibly miss it when I went to brush my teeth. While this one habit has been one of the biggest boosts to my morning, it has an added bonus—within fifteen minutes of waking up, I'm already 25 percent closer to my daily goal of sixty-four ounces. That's a nice little domino.

After my water, I slip into the living room where I light the fireplace and stretch for five minutes. Then I reach for my computer and notes, which are waiting next to my chair where I left them the night before. I take one minute to set my intention and focus my thoughts on what I want to accomplish. And then I start getting into the deep work of writing.

I don't stop until 6:10, when I close the computer, stack up my notes, and make my way to Jack's and Kate's bedrooms to wake them both up before heading back to my room where I slide back into bed for about ten minutes.

Wait. What?

I imagine your furrowed brow, confused at my last statement. It makes no sense. I'm up and ready for my day, and then I go back to bed? But that's what I do. I slip back into my room and into bed next to my husband, who's just beginning to wake up. I call this time my Million Dollar Minutes.

Ten minutes to connect with my husband, to focus with intention on my marriage, before my day begins. We rarely lie there in silence. We usually visit and we always laugh. It doesn't really matter what we do—what matters is that during those minutes, I'm focusing solely on what matters most. I call them Million Dollar Minutes because I know that if this time were gone tomorrow, I would gladly pay a million dollars to get it back. I don't ever want to take this time for granted, so I purposely create that space. You see, *it's not just about managing our time; it's about savoring the moments.*

There are other Million Dollar Minutes in my day—when Kate nestles next to me on the couch wanting to share a playground happening, when Jack plops himself in the back seat after school. These are the times when I know I need to slow down and give my priorities—these people I love—my full attention. If I don't remind myself how valuable these moments are, I'll allow them to slip through my fingers.

The rest of my morning routine is probably very much like yours—getting dressed, calling up the stairs ~~ten~~ twenty-five times to get Jack to stop saying he's out of bed and actually get moving, gathering lunches, signing field trip forms, herding everyone out the door. The day is off and running, but it feels centered because I've started it off with a routine that has meaning for me. You can see in my routine that I take care of myself spiritually, physically, and emotionally.

Now before you roll your eyes and comment that I must have bluebirds flittering alongside my computer chirping happily or mice sewing my dress for the ball, I want to throw in an ice-cold dose of reality. This long morning routine doesn't happen every day. I'm committed to three days a week of this practice because I know there are nights when I may stay up too late or mornings when I wake up and feel too tired to move. If I'm able to do four days? That's a bonus. That flexibility we keep talking about? That's key.

And I feel I have to point this out—I am excited to write this book. I wake up in the morning and think, *I get to write*—not *I have to write*. My heart is on fire with the messages I am sharing. Do you know how hard it is to hit snooze and fall back asleep while your heart is on fire? My mindset makes me want to get up, and that makes all the difference. We will be visiting this idea of perspective later in section 4.

I have a shorter routine for the days when 4:30 a.m. feels, quite frankly, like 4:30 a.m. and I don't even want to think about getting out of bed. My shorter routine retains the important parts—prayer time, my glass of water, my Million Dollar Minutes—and allows me a quicker start to my day. We need to allow for both the ideal *and* the reality.

Routines afford us space and time for what matters to each of us. And because they run on autopilot, we don't have to use up precious brainpower—they just happen. One habit springboarding the next, creating a seamless routine.

———

Like many of us, Brittany feels busy. She works at a four-year school, reads, travels, and has a husband she's crazy about. She shared, though, "Even when I get things done, I still have this deeper yearning for something." When we worked through mapping routines in the liveWELL Method course, she admitted, "I just want to feel like I [do] something meaningful in the morning . . . like I began with unhurried purpose."

I love that phrase she used—*unhurried purpose*. Doesn't that sound like an amazing way for us all to start our days? I pushed her a bit to uncover what would feel meaningful for her. That's the key here: *for her*. Not for me, not for anyone else. What is meaningful for each of us is different. Brittany came back with a four-week plan to focus on feeling hydrated and fit with dedicated time for reading. She laid plans to progress to mixing in affirmations, meditation, and a gratitude journal in later weeks. Speaking about the heart of her routine, she said, "I think I really just need to make space for clarity, quiet, and solitude." It sounds like a beautiful way to start a morning—centered and focused on what matters most.

> **ASK YOURSELF:** What would give meaning to my morning? Take out a sheet of paper and fold it into thirds and title the sections: Spiritual, Emotional, and Physical. Brainstorm and think about what activities could add meaning to your life in these three areas. See if there are ways to create that space or develop a habit you can then build into your morning or evening routine.

AUTOMATIONS MAKE IT HAPPEN

This idea of routine and "taking the thinking out of it" can be applied to all kinds of tasks. Automations are systems for things you don't do every day but need to get done—the minutia.

The word *automation* may sound like technical jargon, but it's not tech at all. It's simply a task that happens automatically without too much thinking. We set up automations because these tasks we do on an irregular basis have a tendency to fall between the cracks, like pennies between our couch cushions. They get pushed aside, to be done "later"—an obscure date sometime in the future—or they are simply forgotten.

When we don't have these tasks scheduled somewhere, they end up getting scheduled nowhere. Suddenly we realize we haven't done laundry in two weeks and no one in the house has clean underwear. Or even a clean shirt (this realization inevitably hits the night before school picture day). Panic takes hold and stress settles in right in its favorite spot at the back of our necks.

This is the moment when a task shifts and transforms into an urgent fire. Everything else, regardless of importance, gets shoved aside to make room to deal with this raging inferno—even if it is just a mountain of dirty clothes.

Remember, we want to be effective. We want to take care of our work so tasks never have a chance to ignite into urgency, but we also want them to happen with as little effort as possible.

Chores are a fabulous task to automate because, let's be honest, who wants to think about chores? No one. But they must be done. As I said at the beginning of section 3, it does us no good to bring home the bacon and fry it up in a pan if the kitchen is burning down around us. We have to keep life moving—even the not-so-glamorous parts.

The problem lies in when we have to burn our calories thinking about these menial tasks and deplete our brainpower so it cannot be used on the truly important items in our day. Decision fatigue loves laundry stress; they're best friends. Let's get our brains working at full capacity and allow ourselves to focus on what's important—which, by the way, is not laundry.

My first home had a tiny section of my kitchen for laundry, and I was frustrated with stepping over clothes while I made dinner. I was teaching school at the time and happened to be teaching a unit on *Little House in the Big Woods*. Funny enough, Laura Ingalls Wilder gave me a solution. She wrote, "Ma said each day had its own proper work . . . Wash on Monday, Iron on Tuesday . . ." and so on. I draw the line at ironing, but Ma was a smart woman. If it worked for her, I decided it would work for me.

I didn't want to start my week with washing, so on Tuesdays I did laundry. And then I had kids. Kids who somehow multiplied my dirty clothes pile by an exponent of twenty. *It defies the rules of math, but it's true.*

Tuesdays remained a laundry day at my house, though. It was the day my kids' clothes were cleaned. When Jack and Kate were littles, around three years old, I began calling up the stairs and saying, "It's Tuesday—laundry day!"

Because it's an automation, they knew this meant they needed to pull their clothes hampers out into the living room before breakfast. I intentionally bought them hampers they could drag to the living room themselves. They didn't have to ask what to do; they just did it because this was the routine.

As my kids got older, around five years old, I built on the routine. They started taking the laundry down and sorting it. I would stand over them

IT DOES US NO GOOD
— TO —

BRING HOME
THE BACON

FRY IT UP IN A PAN
IF THE KITCHEN IS
BURNING DOWN
around you

and guide them. Could I have sorted it faster? Absolutely! But I looked at this as an investment, because soon they were sorting it without my help at all. And as they got older, I built on this routine again and added the next step: they would bring down their laundry, sort it, and then pop it into the machine. No one worried about what needed to be done, no one asked what they should do—it was all automated.

They knew on Tuesdays this was the task to be done. Did they do it without any reminding? I am pretty biased and believe I have amazing kids, but they aren't robots! Of course they needed some prodding and poking from time to time, but life ran much more smoothly because I didn't have to worry about their laundry any other day of the week—laundry simply happened on Tuesdays.

On Fridays we followed a similar automation with laundry for towels and sheets. My kids would strip their beds and bring down their towels, and the whole process repeated for house laundry. I didn't try to tackle everything in one day but spaced it out to alleviate the stress.

By the way, did you notice I shifted to past tense there in that section? Ah, that felt glorious to type out. You know why? Because right now, laundry day is Monday for Kate and Tuesday for Jack. It's changed. Not because their laundry has increased but because they now fully do it themselves. I don't do their laundry at all now because, since they were little, I had been training them. They didn't realize it, but I was investing in them every week, slowly handing over each step of the process.

I know you didn't believe me back in chapter 4 when I said kids could be trained, but it's true. It takes time, yes. It takes investment. My biggest goal, though, is when my little birds leave my nest, they'll fly. And I'm working to give them the tools to do that.

In our CLEAR framework, you'll remember one of the questions is: "Is this advantageous?" *Investing in others takes time but always adds to our advantage.* You know why? My kids have even taken over Friday's house laundry, so when I ask myself if these tasks have to be done by me (*Is it essential?*), the answer is becoming *no* more often.

PUTTING OUR ELEPHANTS ON AUTOPILOT

Automations work in thousands of places at home and at the office: website maintenance, grocery shopping, inventorying, ordering office supplies, dusting. The list goes on and on. We can even use automations to break down tasks that need to be done throughout the year—tasks that we don't do monthly but still need to be done: organizing our closets, checking for expired medications, planning team-building events, surveying customers.

I create a big master list for myself of the tasks and chores I want to accomplish throughout the year. Then at the start of each month, I simply plug these tasks into my calendar. For example, we deep clean the fridge in January, April, July, and October; we go through the medicine cabinet in March and September; we start looking for summer camps in January. As you can see, some tasks happen once and other tasks, like checking for expired medications, happen multiple times a year. Using automations allows us to be proactive—to take tasks that could easily be forgotten and create space for them so they don't slip into urgency mode.

———

Erika has the best laugh of anyone I've ever met. Kind and giving, she works as a director of nursing at a large private school where she dotes on the students like a second mother. She's a born caregiver, but a few years ago she invested some time to start making sure she was taking care of herself by setting up automations. In her words, "I love that automations clear space in my mind so I can focus on other things. Because I simply pop them into my calendar, I can stop worrying about the tasks I need to do and just get them done." The extra bonus was finding that automations helped her feel more present and mindful with her family because "tasks were no longer clogging up [her] brain."

Erika uses automations at home for tasks like changing air filters and fertilizing the yard, but she also uses them to remind her to do the chores most of us forget to do, like cleaning the vacuum filter, disinfecting the washer, and cleaning the dryer vent.

At work Erika uses automations to keep her team of nurses organized so they can spend time caring for their patients instead of focusing on the tedious chores of running a clinic. "I get so excited when I am reminded of an automated task," she told me, "because it makes me feel proud that I set myself up for success. I love my 'past self' at those moments."

We women don't do nearly enough loving on ourselves, I think you will agree. I love that these automations give Erika a moment to pat herself on the back and drop a fresh marble in her jar.

Automations can take our big, overwhelming projects and tasks and make them manageable. One of the other great ways to use automations is to break down bigger tasks into bite-size pieces. Taxes are a great example—we all know taxes are due in April, so why do we wait until the last minute to pull together everything we need? We make a mad-dash scramble to pull our documents together, and then we wonder why we feel grumpy and irritable.

Break the task down and make it easier. In January create a folder with a checklist for the paperwork you are expecting to trickle in over the next few months; in February organize your office area to help uncover any documents that may be helpful for filing; in March make your appointment with your CPA; and in April relax, because your nerves aren't shot from the stress. Set up automations so that each of these pieces of the puzzle is assigned a time and space.

Breaking down big projects, like filing taxes, allows you to eat the elephant and make it feel easier. It also affords you the space to be proactive and do your best work. I use this strategy with our annual redesign of our planners. It's a huge undertaking with all new designs and concepts each year, but we start work nine months before the new designs are due to the printers, giving us room to innovate and explore.

Creating automations allows each task to happen with minimal effort. That's a system that simplifies life and allows it to run with less stress. It's truly being effective.

It's easy to read about these habits, automations, and routines and get caught up in how different they might look from your current daily life. I didn't start here. No one does. Creating these simple systems takes time.

My Christmas Eve dinner wasn't always so smooth—there was the year that I insisted on making a Mexican spread, including a made-to-order quesadilla bar. I spent an entire day caramelizing onions, roasting corn, and prepping about twenty different ingredients for everyone to customize their dinner. During the meal I stood, hungry and cranky, over a hot stove making quesadillas for over an hour while everyone else visited and enjoyed their hot food.

I can tell you, I went to bed that night with more grumbles and complaints than sugarplum dreams. But I admitted I had set myself up with some magazine-worthy ideas that didn't really suit the night I *really* wanted.

My holiday dinner evolved over time. I wanted it to feel special, but I didn't really want fussy. That doesn't suit me. I don't do china plates, I don't do fancy place settings, and I don't do centerpieces.

We've been making the roasted crab now for years, and it's the only day of the year that I do it. The entire meal is eaten without silverware, so it's messy, it's loud, but it feels exactly the way I want it to feel—different from every other day of the year. It's memorable, which is what I *really* wanted all along.

LET ME HELP

Give yourself grace and time to evolve and grow your systems. Know that some will work and others will need adjusting. It's all part of the process. To make this easier for you, I've got a free download to help you begin to think about adding some automations to your life. I've even included a video to make it easier. You can get free access to this bonus feature at joyofmissingout.com/chapter8.

CHAPTER 9

SIMPLIFY STRUCTURE

Sometimes it helps me to wake up in the morning and tell myself, "Today, I'm going to believe that showing up is enough."
BRENÉ BROWN

The thunderous rush of water could be heard long before we approached the bend in the river. The sound of water slapping against the rocks, rolling like a fast-moving snake, roared loudly, warning us of the danger ahead. We were rafting for five days on the Arkansas River, and we were used to the rapids. We had acclimated to the rhythm of the river, but this rapid sounded different. It sounded ferocious and angry. Looking around, I could see the edges of worry on everyone's faces.

Our guide, however, looked blissfully unconcerned as she paddled confidently toward the bank. She lightly hopped out of the raft and motioned for us to follow. Scrambling up a rock face, we stood and viewed the raging river from above. Our guide explained to us that while the boulders don't shift, the river itself is a living thing—each day the water flows in a slightly different pattern, revealing new, menacing obstacles and challenges. With the running of the river that day, she pointed out the hidden rocks that

130

threatened to suck our boat under and several treacherous spots with potential to capsize our group.

Looking at the water from above, the path we should take to safely navigate through the hazards was clear. The river lost its power over us. We confidently made our way to our boat and excitedly sliced our oars into the cool water. Paddling as one, we swirled the boat to the right to avoid the jutting rocks, then dug our paddles in to quickly twist to the left where the river made a gradual drop. Shrieks of laughter pierced the air as we high-fived our successful run. It felt easy—it felt fun.

How did the river go from intimidating to entertaining? All it took was structuring our run. We took some time to create a plan, and suddenly the crushing power of the river didn't seem so out of control. We owned the river that day, and it felt good.

OWN YOUR DAY

We want to own our day, not the other way around. But when we spend all day putting out fires—running from task to task, working through lunch, squeezing in every last drop of the day to get work done—we end our days feeling exhausted and unsatisfied.

Hustle is one of those buzzwords people like to use, especially when it comes to business. In truth, *hustle isn't about business; it's about busyness. Hustle* is just a more aggressive word for *busy*, meaning "to jostle" and "to crowd and push roughly"—and often what we crowd is our day. We jam-pack our schedule from start to finish with activities, tasks, projects, and errands. We don't give ourselves the space to breathe.

Despite what social media tells us, *life is not about the hustle.* But we have this learned helplessness that tells us we cannot own our day, that it does not truly belong to us. If this is true, who does our day belong to? Our bosses? Our families? Other people who push their agendas and priorities on us that we accept out of guilt?

Remember our locus of control we talked about in chapter 2? Let's build it back up and remind ourselves that we are in charge. Because when we feel in control of our schedule, we don't just survive; we thrive.

Creating structure for our days can be beautifully simple and takes only minimal effort. Like all good systems, the effort is small but the rewards are great. I've created a system that you can easily personalize and customize to you and your life called the 5 Ps of planning:

We need to be present in our lives, accountable for where our day takes us and responsible for our choices. Without presence, productivity can become busyness, where we find ourselves performing task after task that has little meaning to us in the long run. When we can act upon our North Star on a daily basis, accomplishments will follow.

Being present simply requires filtering out the minutia, purposely choosing not to do everything, and instead intentionally planning our day. That's where a system like the 5 Ps helps make it easier to focus on what's important. Let's unpack this together and go through each of these steps.

PURGE

We have to take the thinking out of it. Doing so is key to all good systems, and planning is no different. We have short-term working memory that allows us to focus on the information we need to successfully complete our tasks. This memory, though, is limited and can easily be overloaded with too much information.

When everything we need to accomplish is swirling around in our heads, it can take up a lot of space. Space we need to complete our tasks instead of fretting or stressing about whether we'll remember to do the task!

Studies show that our work suffers when we have distracting thoughts, and just like decision fatigue, distraction wears out the brain.

Using our brains like giant filing cabinets for our tasks is simply not effective. Purging our task list from our heads creates the space we need. It's as easy as doing a brain dump so we can move it out of our brains and onto some paper.

This first step in the 5 Ps is taking time to think through the entire week. We can look ahead at the big picture of what we want to accomplish over the next seven days. I do a weekly purge on Sundays for my home and on Mondays for work. I purposely keep these planning sessions separate because I want to make sure that in my head, these two sections have their own boundaries and space.

This first step—purging—can take place on your own or with a team. Most of us know what planning alone looks like, so I'll share with you how I do this first step for home tasks with my family.

Every Sunday afternoon we have an automation called "team planning." You see, we refer to our family as Team Dalton. We started this when our kids were very little to help build a sense of unity for the four of us. We all work together to make things happen, and if one member doesn't do their share, the whole team can fall apart. Team planning reinforces this for us.

The four of us sit around our kitchen table and brainstorm everything we need to do or accomplish in the week ahead: homework, chores, meals, sports practices, and so on. You can do this on a sheet of blank paper, but I have a notepad called the Weekly Kickstart that is designed to help make this first step even easier. There's room for us to write down our brain dump list, and it has space to plug in any timed appointments (like dentist appointments or carpool times). This then becomes our master list, which I post in a prominent place in our kitchen for everyone to reference.

Every one of us is responsible for making our team work. My family knows to check the Weekly Kickstart to see what needs to happen (when they need to be ready to go for activities, what chores need to be completed, and so on). They don't need to ask me, and I don't have to use up precious brainpower reminding them. Even when my kids were little and couldn't read, we used this system. I would use stickers and drawings to convey tasks, and I set up a digital clock so they always knew the time. I'm setting up my little birds to fly, and this is one of the ways I do that.

This first step of planning not only helps life run smoothly but it can also begin to feel like a beautiful tradition.

Kim, in my Facebook group, is in a high-stress time of life. She's working on her graduate degree and has recently dealt with a big life change of moving. She shared,

> I love planning at the beginning of the week by making it a ritual. Grab some coffee or tea, look at my goals—what actions can I take to keep moving forward? Maybe listen to a podcast or review notes from one and find something I can put into practice. I love it because it makes me feel centered.

For Kim, taking the time to think ahead, which is what we are doing when we complete this first step, helps her feel more focused on the life she wants to live. Planning doesn't have to feel too rigid or constraining—it can become a highlight of your week if you allow it.

PROCESS

PURGE > **PROCESS** > PRIORITIZE > PROTECT > PROPEL

What we don't want to do, though, is make our daily lists during weekly planning. One of the biggest mistakes I see people make is planning out the entire week in one sitting, slotting in what they'll do Friday afternoon even though it's still six days away. They purge but don't take the time to follow up with step two: process.

We need to process each day as it comes, making a daily plan for the greatest impact. This is the secret to making our days achievable. Why? Because let's say Monday is a great start to the week. You feel good and have a productive day. But then Tuesday happens. Tuesday starts out with a child crawling into your bed at 3:00 a.m., followed by a morning with you downing allergy meds like Tic Tacs thanks to the pollen in the air. Your head feels like it's chockablock full of cotton, and you never seem to recover.

Unfortunately, if you've already planned every single day of your week, Wednesday opens with you feeling ten steps behind because you have to make up for that hot mess of a Tuesday. You have Tuesday *and* Wednesday tasks to complete. You feel underwater and it's not even 8:00 a.m. Before you know it, it's Thursday and it feels like you'll never get ahead.

We need to treat each day like a new opportunity. Some days will be amazing and we'll get twice as much accomplished as we hoped, and some days, well, some days are just Tuesdays. And that's okay.

The purge we do at the start of the week gives us a bird's-eye view of what we want to accomplish, so we need to pull from this list to process what we want to accomplish each day. Ten minutes at the start of every day to focus solely on *that* day gives us the grace and flexibility we need for those "Tuesday mornings."

Break down the big tasks and choose what is most important to get done, and then focus only on those steps you can accomplish today. Think through your energy level, mood, and expectations, and then set your intention for what you will accomplish that day—and that day only. *That's the biggest secret to setting ourselves up for success: making sure our days are actually achievable.*

We want to make sure our daily list doesn't just focus on the urgent tasks; we want to ensure consistent movement toward our North Star by spending time cultivating the important work—the tasks without a screaming deadline. Similar to eating our elephant, we can break down the bigger goals for our week and work consistently throughout our days to move us closer. Build up small wins, start small to build momentum, and use the confidence you build from those small wins to move you on to bigger tasks.

Think about it: If your goal was to run a marathon, you wouldn't go out and run all 26.2 miles—you would start with one. It's the same with your daily tasks. Take your time to determine the steps that are achievable today. I think that's the big issue—we often set ourselves up for failure by putting far too much on our plates. We have to ask ourselves: *What can I accomplish* today? It's okay to start small and allow your capacity to grow. *Small steps are better than no steps.*

Take your goals and break them down into monthly pieces, which can be broken down into weekly focuses, which then can be broken down even further into daily actions—small steps. I believe so strongly in connecting with your goals each month that I designed my inkWELL Press planners with Monthly Mission Boards to help you check in and keep you heading toward your North Star.

Jennifer is a writer and editor who dreams of starting her own business. Like all of us, she has a thousand things pulling on her every day. She has found success, though, through regular checks-ins using the Monthly Mission Board. In my Facebook group, she shared, "I use the focus [area] to break down my monthly goals into weekly tasks. . . . I jot down tasks that need to get done that week." Then she pulls from her weekly task list—her purge list—and focuses on what she can accomplish each day.

One of her goals is to tap into her love of reading by making time for two books each month. She was happy to report, "I've exceeded that goal every month." To help her stay on track, Jennifer said, "I divide up the number of chapters by the number of weekdays and use the habit tracker . . . to keep me honest on reading one to two chapters a day."

If we make small steps every day toward our bigger goals, toward the life we want for ourselves, that's where happiness lies.

For me, processing is simply an extension of my morning routine—it's a habit. Every day, once I arrive at my office, I begin with ten minutes of focused processing time. Before checking in with email, before other people have the opportunity to fill my calendar with their priorities—first things first. I draw from my purge list on my Weekly Kickstart, choosing the tasks I plan to accomplish that day, and plug them into my planner.

Taking the time to process and select our daily tasks sets us up for success. It allows us to be present and accountable, and it keeps us moving toward our North Star.

PRIORITIZE

We can use the CLEAR framework and the priority list as our guide to structure our day. I want you to start giving yourself permission to prioritize the work that will move you forward. If we are hyperfocused solely on results, we can lose sight of our North Star. Opportunities for growth and learning are often seen as an indulgence because they focus on the long-term benefits rather than immediate results, but this is the work that will ultimately drive us toward our ideal life. This is the important work we need to prioritize more.

We have to limit the amount of time we are giving unimportant items. And, yes, I used the term *giving* here very intentionally. We are gifting time to tasks and activities as if our time were infinite and we can generously hand it all away.

We will always have tasks under *Accommodate* on our list, but we have to make sure to contain them. We can't let them dictate our day. We need to own our day—and the first step is taking charge like you are the boss of your time . . . because you are. Even if you don't think you are the boss, *you* own your time. As Greg McKeown said, "If you don't prioritize your life, someone else will."

One of my favorite systems to help create space in my day is batching. Batching is intentionally collecting similar activities for an intentional block of time to maximize time, energy, and focus. Did you notice a word appearing again and again? Batching our tasks is working with *intention*. And if we are working with intention, it means we are focusing on priorities—we are getting important work done.

This is true even if we batch unimportant tasks because then these *distractions* are done at one time, allowing us to spend the majority of our time on our priorities. It helps declutter our days. Instead of doing the same tasks again and again, we streamline them and do them in fewer sessions so they disrupt less of our day. I'll show you what I mean:

When we create larger pockets for important work, we accomplish more in our day.

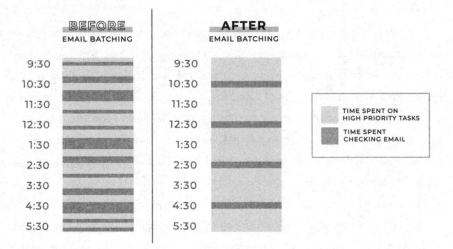

One of my podcast listeners, Vinnilaa from Malaysia, works full-time and juggles the roles of wife, mom, worker, daughter-in-law, and more, making her feel stretched thin. But, by batching her tasks, she shared, "I accomplish a lot more tasks than before and at the end of the day, I feel so happy. Batching tasks gave me extra time to have ME time."

Tasks, whether important or not, can be batched together two ways:

BY ACTION: grouped by similar activities: repetitive tasks like calls or emails, reading, packaging products

BY CONTEXT: grouped by situations, tools, or surroundings: prepping lunches for the week, running errands, writing blog posts

Once we group our activities together, we can set aside an amount of time to work on the batched tasks. I call this amount of time a container—it gives me boundaries and a structure from which I can work and tells me when I need to walk away. This is key, especially when batching unimportant tasks.

Batching works with the way our brains work: it moves with our ultradian rhythm, so it uses our energy effectively. It takes over twenty minutes for the brain to get into the zone of doing deeper work. Batching allows us to get into that elusive flow, a deeper state of thinking, so we get higher-quality work using less time. Sounds like the definition of being effective, doesn't it?

PROTECT

PURGE   PROCESS   PRIORITIZE   PROTECT   PROPEL

Over the last eight chapters I've been preaching to you about not filling your day, but now I'm going tell you just the opposite. I'm warning you because I don't want you to think I've lost it—just stick with me here and I'll explain. Ready?

I want you to fill your calendar. Fill it up in the morning during your process time, slot in your important tasks, schedule your batches, block your time. Use your ultradian rhythm as your guide to make sure you block off time for focus and time for breaks.

Why do we want to do this? Because *we* want to fill our calendars first. A wide-open calendar is an invitation for others to cram it full with their priorities and demands rather than our own.

Let's fill our calendar with our priorities before we allow others access to our time. This helps us establish our boundaries and allows us to "burn the boats" just as Archimedes did. Focused blocks of work get placed in your daily agenda first, followed by breaks.

Block out sections of time for you to work on priority items or batched tasks. Higher-ranking priorities should get the lion's share of your time, so block off those items first in your calendar. These are nonnegotiable time blocks that belong to you, so treat them as you would an appointment with someone else—you wouldn't cancel your doctor's appointment or arrive thirty minutes late. Right? This is an appointment with you and your goals.

Here's the catch: to time block effectively, we need to be careful not to line up our blocks one right after the other. We need to allow for some buffers so there's some breathing room—to allow for the expansion of ideas. Similar to when we drive our cars, we don't tailgate and ride the bumper of the car in front of us (at least, I hope we don't). We give ourselves a buffer of space to allow for sudden braking or swerves in the road.

Giving ourselves buffers provides us the flexibility we need to be pro-active. The solution can be as easy as giving yourself a 50 percent buffer. If it takes you ten minutes to get to the soccer fields, leave the house fifteen minutes before you need to get there. You'll feel less stressed and flustered, and if you arrive early, you can take that time and spend it on something you like to do: read a book for five minutes, call your mom, or do whatever makes you happy. I consider this a hidden pocket of time in which I have focused conversations with my kids—no distractions. It's amazing the deep connections we can make when we strip away everything else.

Buffers give us the flexibility we need so our systems don't fail. Remember in the last chapter when I talked about my laundry automation? Tuesday was laundry day, but do you know when my kids put away their clothes? Tuesday? Definitely not. Wednesday's automation for my kids was putting away their clothes.

A WIDE-OPEN CALENDAR
IS AN *invitation* FOR OTHERS
TO CRAM IT FULL WITH THEIR
PRIORITIES & DEMANDS
RATHER THAN OUR OWN

Let's be honest with ourselves and realize that not every Tuesday is made of rainbows and lollipops. I gave myself and my family the space to allow grace for those Tuesdays that didn't feel smooth. You know, the Tuesdays when the last load went in right before bedtime?

Finishing the laundry on Wednesday meant we never felt like we failed. If we happened to get laundry done and put away on Tuesday? Bonus! But putting it away on Wednesday was still a win. When we create tight time-lines for ourselves, the margin for success is razor thin, and then we feel like we've failed because we didn't stick to our schedules—*even if no one is holding us to our schedules but ourselves*. Let's set ourselves up for success by allowing ourselves the room we need.

PROPEL

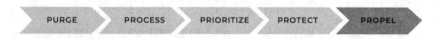

The last step in this system is what I consider one of the most important —we need to give ourselves a little *velocity*. We need to set up our dominoes.

When asked about finding inspiration, Ernest Hemingway said, "As long as you can start, you are all right." He recommended that, "The important thing is to have good water in the well." Hemingway's idea of leaving water in the well means we never want to leave a task or a project without knowing how we will pick it back up. We want to return to our tasks with the same momentum, so when we leave a task unfinished, we simply need to take a moment to leave some water in our wells.

You saw some evidence of the water I leave in my well in chapter 8. I shared my morning routine, and I mentioned my computer sitting next to my chair. Every night before heading to bed, I plug in my computer so it's fully charged when I get up. Stacked on top are my glasses and notes for what I need to do next. Knowing my computer is there waiting reduces the energy I need to start. It's a little domino that helps get my morning moving.

We can use this idea in all areas of our day to help build momentum:

leaving lunch items ready to assemble on the counter after cleaning up dinner, keeping backpacks by the back door where they won't be forgotten in the hubbub of the morning, placing a note in your planner with next-action items.

When it comes to leaving water in the well, one of my favorite methods is to create a dedicated folder for projects. You can create a project log to staple on the inside flap of the folder where you write out the date, time spent, and next steps. The benefit of this is not only the water in the well but also the bread crumb trail of what you've accomplished. This helps you see how much time you spent on the project (which will help you with planning in the future), and you'll get a feeling of accomplishment for what you've done. I think bread crumbs are important because many of us undervalue the amount of time we've spent—always thinking we haven't done enough or didn't work hard enough. It's hard, though, to argue with data; bread crumbs show you your success.

This is why I believe the Daily Download adds significant water to your well. This five-minute activity is responsible for doubling my productivity, and I believe in it so strongly that I created a special notepad for it.* The framework of it is simple, though; you can even use a sheet of paper if you'd like.

> **MINUTE ONE** is spent reflecting on our accomplishments for the day. I find, at the end of the day, it's hard to think of all the good we've done, so taking one minute to reflect makes a huge difference. In fact, one study found that when employees spent a few minutes at the end of the workday reflecting on their day, they saw a 23 percent increase in their performance levels. It's important to count the marbles in our jars.

> **MINUTE TWO** is focused on evaluating our day. Did we put too much on our plate? How was our stress? Our attitude? Our focus? This

---

* You can view the notepad and all the inkWELL Press products mentioned in this chapter at inkwellpress.com/jomo.

allows us to make certain we are setting up achievable days. If we consistently score high on stress and low on attitude, we need to make some adjustments.

MINUTE THREE is for assessing what you did to move closer to accomplishing your goals. Check in and ask yourself each day to assess how you are inching closer to your North Star. A little progress each day makes a difference.

MINUTE FOUR is all about gratitude. Find three things you are grateful for every day. The trick is, it needs to be specific to that day. For example, "I am grateful for lunch with Susan because she helped me feel confident about my project." According to happiness expert Shawn Achor, if you do this for twenty-one days, you'll set a pattern of low-level optimism, even if you think you are naturally a pessimist.

MINUTE FIVE is for setting up our dominoes. Write down a few notes about tomorrow's action items—the important tasks you would like to focus on the following day. Get them out of your head and down on paper. It's important to recognize we aren't planning our tomorrow; we are simply giving ourselves guidance on what we can work on next—a little water in our well.

Structuring our time and filling our calendars full of priorities for ourselves requires courage because it means we are clearly marking our boundaries. It means we are intentionally missing out on the rest of the noise that adds clutter and chaos to our lives.

Our days can rush past like the fast-moving currents of the river while challenges and obstacles seem to appear from nowhere. But if we take the time to scout our paths, if we give ourselves the gift of structure and design our lives to work for us, we will be free to enjoy the ride, even when it gets a little bumpy. Let's enjoy the journey while we paddle downriver—I'm ready to slap you a high-five when we make it through those rapids.

ACHIEVE HARMONY

Harmonize your life by letting go of balance and shifting your life toward your goals and dreams.

Over the last three sections, we have been laying the groundwork to turn your ideal life into your everyday life. Everything we have worked toward culminates in this fourth and final step of the liveWELL Method. We will build upon the new foundation and processes we have created and pull it all together to create harmony so you can live the beautiful, purposeful life you deserve.

My intention for this next section is for you to understand why it's important to have whitespace in our lives. This space is imperative for us to be able to give ourselves fully to others. We will use an easy-to-follow blueprint for finding *your* yes and feeling better about saying no. We will jettison the idea of balance and begin to shift our mindset so we can stop looking at our lives as these 24-hour snapshots and instead see the harmony of the 168 hours we all get each week.

CHAPTER 10

HARMONIZE WHITESPACE

The world will see you the way you see you,
and treat you the way you treat yourself.
BEYONCÉ

My son, Jack, has stopped calling me Mommy.

There was no fanfare, no confetti, no bells going off the moment he chose to stop using that title with me. I have no idea what day was "the last day." He called down the stairs to me—I don't recall what he asked me, but I do clearly remember that he called me *Mom*. I looked over at John and said, "He called me Mom." I sat there a little dumbfounded.

And I wondered, *When did this happen?* So I flipped through the card catalog in my brain (is it just me who imagines myself flipping through cards of information until I finally hold the right one up triumphantly?) and started feverishly tearing apart the stacks, scouring for moments when he'd referred to me as Mommy. I realized it had apparently been a while.

This is a good thing, I have to remind myself. Jack is, after all, a teenager—I should have known this was going to happen. It would be strange for a high school kid to call his mother *Mommy*. And let's be honest, I wouldn't want him at the age of thirty referring to me as Mommy.

It does make me think—we don't know when the last time for any-thing will happen. Let's make the most of these moments and slow down to enjoy them. *We have to stop rushing through life and missing all the good-ness that is there before us.* We need to create space to soak in and enjoy the moments.

OWN YOUR CIRCUS

We've all experienced that vague sense of dissatisfaction with our day. Time passes in a blur as we sit at our desks without really paying attention to the tasks or even the people around us. We punch the clock, getting work done, but when the day closes we feel like we accomplished nothing. This is why we feel unsatisfied when we lay our heads on our pillows, why we wonder where the day has gone.

We complain we've got a million things to do, that our lives are like a circus. Only instead of flame eaters, jugglers, and sword swallowers in every ring, we've got overloaded schedules, overcommitted kids, and overbooked weekends. We've created our own circuses and we wonder why the clowns are running around with their hair on fire.

Let's allow this to sink in for a minute, though. We are the ones who raised our hands to volunteer for the charity event, we are the ones who signed up our kids for ten weeks straight of out-of-town soccer tourna-ments, we are the ones who are spending our weekends aiming to win the Yard of the Month. We own that circus.

We are doing our very best, I know, but we can live better. We can live happier, but doing more won't achieve this. In trying to chase down balance, we are trying to do it all. We are spreading ourselves paper thin.

I've said it before and I'll say it again: balance is bogus. Balance doesn't exist, and we don't *want* it to exist. If all things are balanced, there can be no movement or growth—everything would stand still. There is magic in the unbalanced because that's when we begin to move forward. We need counterbalance to make our lives work—we need harmony.

CREATE YOUR OWN HARMONY

Harmony can be found in the 168 hours we have each week, but so many people choose to focus—almost hawklike—on just the 24 hours of each day. Twenty-four hours is such a tiny snapshot of the whole picture, literally one-seventh of our week. And yet each day is treated as if it stands alone, so there's a tendency to look at this tiny snapshot as our chance at achieving this mythical balance.

This means all our priorities—all the things that matter the most—have to squeeze in and find time during this small window. Time management expert Laura Vanderkam calls this the "24-Hour Trap" because it's simply not feasible. She shares, "Any given 24 hours might not be balanced, but the 168-hour week as a whole can be." In other words, we have to stop looking at our lives as individual days and begin to look at the bigger picture.

When we zoom out and look at the week as a whole, we can begin to find harmony in unexpected places. We need to stop treating each day as its own scorecard to be checked for balance. Look at your week as a whole and see if maybe you are spending more time on your priorities than you realize. We have a tendency to beat ourselves up and to notice only the things we didn't do well, when in reality we are doing much better than we think.

If we view the week as seven opportunities for success, we have a greater chance of achieving harmony. Look at time requirements with fresh eyes too. If we have a priority tugging on us because it feels like an impossible dream, we need to get creative with our thinking.

Let's talk about a common balance complaint: "I work too much and never seem to make it home for dinner with the family." We feel like our balance is out of whack and we must be doing something wrong.

If you have a job that requires occasional late hours or you travel for work, making it home for dinner every single night will be difficult. By setting yourself up for this rigid expectation of five nights a week, you are setting yourself up for failure. On the nights you don't make it home, it's easy to believe you have failed.

If you choose, instead, to look at the harmony of 168 hours, you might notice that while you didn't make it home for dinnertime on Wednesday, you did spend time together on Sunday, Monday, Thursday, and even Friday. You were together four evenings out of seven.

Why don't we zoom it out even further, though? Let's get to the heart of why dinner with the family is a priority. For most people, it's not about the act of sitting down and eating at the end of the day that's important. It's the intentional time spent together that matters. So who says this has to happen around the dinner table? Could meaningful time happen in the morning? Is it possible to go into work a little bit later so you can have some time together before work happens? Or could you scoot away from the office and schedule in a lunch once a week with your family? What about weekends? If work keeps you burning the midnight oil during the workweek, can you schedule in some very intentional blocks of focused family time on the weekend?

The priority is enjoying time together as a family. We need to loosen up our narrow definition of how we spend time on our priorities. When we do that, harmony can flourish.

Remember the Squirrel Strategy from chapter 2? Let's look at our weeks using this same strategy:

> *Need to do a lot of networking for your job? Who says it has to happen at happy hour? Why not try hosting some coffee meet-ups in the morning or midafternoon?*

> *Don't think you have time for date night with your spouse? Try meeting once or twice a month for lunch dates while the kids are in school. Maybe even throw in the occasional lunch at a hotel where you get sandwiches from room service and some "exercise."*

> *No time for your favorite pastimes, such as reading? Carry your current read with you everywhere you go, and then grab those hidden pockets of time while standing in line at the grocery store or while waiting for piano lessons to be over. That's how Stephen King reads*

five hours every single day while still publishing bestselling fiction of his own.

My point being, there are a thousand ways we can make our priorities sit front and center when we get creative. We just have to treat our priorities as priorities.

YOU DO HAVE THE TIME

We have to stop telling ourselves that we simply don't have the time. If we are serious about creating space in our day, we need look no further than our calendars. When we look at our time in these 168-hour weekly blocks, and we allot 8 hours of sleep at night, we are left with 112 waking hours. Then, if we deduct our 40-hour workweek, we discover that we have 72 hours left. Seventy-two hours for us to choose how to spend—we can spend it in ways that we *really* want, or we can continue running a circus. Ultimately the choice is ours.

It's all about effectiveness over efficiency. It's not about micromanaging your clock so you become ten seconds more efficient at checking email. It's stepping back and deciding whether those emails are important in the first place. If not, why are you filling so much of your day with them? Batch that task so it's not a distraction. Give yourself permission to focus on what's truly important. Time management is not about learning how to do things faster; it's choosing where—and how—to spend your time.

———

Kali* is one of the brightest women I know, with born leadership qualities and an absolute passion for her work. She's the type of person who thrives on big projects, complicated timelines, and managing teams. Over the past

---

* Name has been changed.

few years, since leaving her job to be at home, she has lost the shine in her eyes, her smile seems harder to come by, and her excitement for life itself seems to have waned. Knowing her love of her work, I pressed her about why she quit.

She admitted that her kids' schedules were just too demanding—there was simply no way she could work. Both her kids were active in sports, one was taking acting lessons, the other was on a dance team, both were learning violin—the list of activities went on and on. She told me her afternoons were packed full to the brim. Weekends weren't any better with the kids' travel soccer teams. Traveling and sitting through game after game made her feel exhausted.

So I asked her, "If sitting at soccer tournaments all weekend long isn't fulfilling and makes family time feel stressed, why are you choosing to enroll your kids in so many activities?" She looked at me like I was crazy and replied, "It's not a choice. I don't want them to be behind everyone else."

We are so committed to making sure our kids don't miss out on any opportunities that we cram their schedules full to the point of bursting like overfilled water balloons. But have we stopped to ask if that's what *they* really want? Have we stopped to ask if that's what *we* really want? Or do we just continue doing it because that's what we are supposed to do? Everyone else has their kids enrolled, so we should too.

This, my friend, is just another story we are telling ourselves. *A good parent makes sure their kid never misses out*—even if it means we are spending our entire afternoon speeding from one activity to the next, missing dinner as a family, and falling into bed at night, drained and frazzled.

Here's a hard truth for us to accept—we are *choosing* this. And if we choose it, then we need to own it. It's our circus—complete with the juggling clowns. Stop complaining about it, stop fussing that there's no time, because we are choosing this lifestyle for ourselves whether we mean to or not.

It's easy, though, to understand why this happens.

WE NEED TO SLEEP LIKE A SHARK

"I'm like a shark—I have to keep moving. If I stop, I die."

Those words were tossed out lightheartedly by a good friend of mine recently during a call. We were discussing all the never-ending tasks and events filling up our days. I laughed when she said it, but her phrase stuck with me long after we hung up.

We all feel busy—overbusy, if we're being honest—and we feel as if that's normal life. It's what everyone does—just scroll through your social media feed. It seems like everyone is doing it all and, according to their camera roll, doing it well. We are under an extraordinary amount of pressure to keep up that pace.

And that's created a lot of sharks in the water—people who think that if they dare to stop moving, if they quit rushing from one task to the next, they will just cease to exist. They will lose their importance—their place in the world.

Sharks glide through the salty water at the top of the food chain, but they are burdened with the constant task of movement. For sharks to breathe, oxygen-rich water must continually flow over their gills. Their fins act like the wings of a fighter jet, giving them lift. If a shark stops moving, it will sink to the sandy bottom of the ocean floor and suffocate. Sharks are predators in constant motion, which has led scientists for years to wonder, *If sharks can never stop moving, how do they sleep?*

It wasn't until a recent expedition to Guadalupe Island that the mystery was solved. Scientists were tracking a large great white shark named Emma. During the daylight hours they watched as she stayed deep in the warm waters, stalking her prey swimming above. But as night fell, Emma's behavior began to drastically shift. She settled her giant body near the sandy bottom of the shallow waters and placed herself directly into the oncoming current. With jaws gaping open, she appeared to go into a sleeplike state. The swift current passed effortlessly over her gills, keeping her alive while allowing her to slow down and conserve her energy.

If the ocean's apex predator can learn to slow herself down to allow some time for rest, surely we can too. This is an animal that truly cannot stop moving, and yet she's found a way to recharge. This downtime, this whitespace, is important for the shark to thrive. We need that too.

When we are busy, there's very little time for quiet—the noise begins to feel so natural, we don't even notice it. And then, when we finally do have some quiet, it can be unsettling because we've gotten so used to the steady hum. But this is the whitespace you want—strike that—it's the whitespace you *need* so you can dive deep into who you really are and who you want to be.

CARVING OUT TIME FOR YOU

When we think about being productive, we believe we need to fill our day completely so we can do as much as possible. In reality, *to be truly productive we need to give our brains a little space to play and explore*—some unstructured time.

And I get it. We feel like we can't disconnect—it's become an expectation to turn around emails and texts at all hours. We've lost sight of our own boundaries. Before smartphones, we clocked out on the weekends, we weren't expected to always be available 365 days a year, and we could go on vacation without worrying whether our bosses were going to call. Smartphones are designed to connect us, but rather than pulling us closer to those we love, they are chaining us to our work. We have to choose to carve out space.

I know what you might be saying to yourself. *I don't have time to play. Other people do, but not me. Who has time for play?* But I would challenge you and tell you that we all have time for whitespace. We do. We have spaces of time in our schedule already—we just don't purposefully carve them out. And because we don't create this space with intention, we aren't reaping the full benefits of our whitespace. I'll show you what I mean:

Raise your hand if, in the last twelve months, you have binge-watched a TV show or taken a silly online quiz, maybe to find out which character in Star Wars you are most like or which Hogwarts house you belong in. If you chased away boredom by playing a mindless game on your phone, your hand should be up too. I'm betting we all have our hands raised (and, yes, mine included—after all, I know I was sorted into Ravenclaw).

We have the time, but the idea of intentionally creating space for this unstructured time feels uncomfortable. It feels silly because we are grown-ups and we don't think we need recess. But we do. Whitespace is essential for our own well-being.

If we don't purposely carve out this space, our brain automatically fills it with meaningless tasks like checking our phones and social media, which can feel like a good way to distract ourselves in the moment but doesn't help us in the long run. Recent studies show that the average person will spend five years and four months of their life on social media. What could we do with that time instead? Well, you know that marathon you've been saying you want to run but just don't have the time for? In those five years you could run *hundreds* of marathons.

Recently we went on a five-day whitespace vacation with my best friend's family—and absolutely no technology. Two families: four full-time working parents, two tween girls, two teenage boys, and zero devices. None. Crazy, right? You know what happened, though? Our kids sat up late and had deep conversations with one another, they collected grasshoppers in a Pringles can, they studied ants gathering together cracker crumbs for two hours. They laughed. They interacted.

For five glorious days we were all untethered from our computers, from our televisions, from our phones. During this whitespace, I realized we are often so focused on our screens we forget to look around. We forget to interact with the world around us—we don't look up; we walk, eyes down, hunched over our phones like addicts. We have lost the ability to truly connect. Connect with others *and* connect with ourselves.

We have to turn off the phone so we aren't tempted to peek at the screen, we have put our email on pause (you know you can do that, right?), and we have to trust that our teams at work can carry on without us checking in on them again and again. The bonus of disconnecting is that it helps ensure our systems are working and it empowers our teams to feel confident in making choices and moving forward on work without us. That is a good thing.

STAKE YOUR BOUNDARIES

Boundaries are key when it comes to creating this space. We have to carve out this time for ourselves because it will not magically appear unless we put in some effort.

Kelly, a student in my liveWELL Method course, is a great mom who struggles with the many roles a single parent has to play. It's not easy being the sole provider and being in charge of everything at work and home. It's easy to forget to take time for yourself. Kelly shared, "My boundaries for self-care always go by the wayside when I don't feel like I did enough to earn the time."

I don't think Kelly is alone in feeling this way, so I challenged her by asking, "When *do* you feel you've earned the time?" I was curious because for most people, the feeling of having done enough is like pouring water into a bucket with a hole in it—it's never filled.

Kelly decided to track her time and discovered that her problem wasn't whether she had done enough; it was whether she *appeared* to do enough. She realized she "was so focused on if other . . . people thought [she'd] put enough hours in at the office." It wasn't about her own expectations but her feeling that others didn't think she had a right to that time.

I know you are nodding your head with me here as we realize that this is yet another story we are telling ourselves. But the beauty of acknowledging our stories is that we have the ability to rewrite our own endings. A few weeks later, Kelly shared this win:

Woo Hoo! Today I sent the kids to play outside for 15 minutes after dinner while I sat down and read a book! For pleasure! I decided after completing an awesome meeting and taking care of my girls it was ENOUGH. I deserved it.

I think my favorite part is that last sentence: *I deserved it*. She does deserve it, and so do you, but often our inner critic tells us otherwise. It barks loudly at us, telling us we should be busy and reminding us we have to achieve certain tasks to be worthy. It's the voice that tells us anything we do for ourselves is selfish. But giving space to ourselves is self-care, and self-care isn't selfish.

AM I BEING SELFISH?

That word *selfish* comes up all the time when I start talking with women about making room for ourselves. We are taught by society—by our upbringing—to be givers. We give, we give, we give, and we feel guilty taking.

Guilt lies in wait, lurking around the dark corners of our brain with an air of superiority. When opportunities arise, it swiftly stands and rushes to whisper in our ear reminders of why we are not worthy. And then with a curved, cruel smile, it snakes its way back to the shadowy nooks to wait again for more prey.

When it comes to taking time for ourselves, when we allow ourselves to recharge and recenter, our guilt stops whispering and begins to shout. You might be wrestling with this concept of giving space and time to yourself because it challenges so much of what you know about who you are and your role in this world.

You are a giver, I know. You love to give to others, even at the expense of yourself. If I were there next to you, I would take your hand at this moment and look you in the eye and tell you this truth: when we make time for our wants and needs, we are able to give our fullest selves to the world around us.

The things that matter—like love, happiness, and compassion—need to be cultivated in your own life before you can make a difference in the

WHEN WE MAKE TIME
FOR OUR
WANTS AND NEEDS
WE ARE ABLE TO GIVE OUR

FULLEST SELVES

·TO THE WORLD AROUND US·

world by extending those feelings to others. John Maxwell said it best when he reminded us, "To bring out the best in others, I first have to bring out the best in me. I cannot give what I do not have." This is a mantra I often need to put on repeat in my own head.

If we do not have compassion for ourselves, how can we give it willingly to others? If we don't treat ourselves with love, how can we truly love others?

We speak to ourselves in hurtful, angry tones. We hurl insults—things we would never say aloud to anyone else—but we think nothing of saying these poisonous words to ourselves. The grace we give to others greatly exceeds the grace we offer ourselves.

I understand that the idea of self-care can feel a little too warm and fuzzy for some people. If you are like me, you were taught when you fell down to "rub a little dirt on it and get back up." There's nothing wrong with that, but we do need to make sure we allow for some self-compassion too.

Self-care is important and as soft as the idea may seem, there's a lot of hard evidence to back it up. There are studies proving it increases our problem-solving abilities, research showing it helps us bounce back after adversity, and evidence affirming it even increases self-motivation.

Get the idea? In other words, when we practice self-compassion, it boosts our overall satisfaction with life (and yes, I have a study to prove that one too). It's important to take care of you.

> **ASK YOURSELF:** When we are satisfied with life, doesn't that bleed into all the areas of our world? How we treat our families? How we connect with our friends? How we interact with strangers on the street?

Being mindful and taking time to give yourself the space you need is an investment in yourself. I think so many women struggle with this because whitespace might feel like a waste of time—after all, you aren't running around and doing things. You are being still.

But giving yourself whitespace and taking care of yourself isn't a luxury, and it's not pampering. It's essential to higher productivity, creativity, and concentration. Because our brains are constantly stimulated, giving ourselves space allows us to do our best work. It seems counterintuitive, but space allows for increased focus. *Whitespace is where ideas, innovation, and ideals are born and nurtured.*

Remember the CLEAR framework? That came about as a result of whitespace. I had been struggling with how to talk to others about what is important. I was finding that, again and again, people would come to me frustrated, wondering how they could discern what needed to be on their priority list. I was stumped, to be honest, because how *do* you tell others what is important—especially when the answer is different for everyone?

I decided to wrestle with the issue on a three-hour plane trip. To make sure I didn't get off track, I put nothing in my carry-on but my notebook and pen. No book to tempt me to read, no computer to lure me to work. I had nothing but a notebook, a pen, and three hours of whitespace.

I sat on the plane with an open notebook and an open mind. By the time the wheels of the plane hit the tarmac, I had designed a model for how to define what is important. The CLEAR framework was born from that open space because I was able to let my brain explore.

Our lives are a series of moments, one after the other, that we can fill with being busy. Or we can try using a few of these moments to be still and silent, allowing ourselves to grow and find deeper meaning. This is when the quiet voice inside our head whispers to us so softly we must strain to hear it. When we don't make this space and allow this quiet voice to be heard, we feel disruption. We wonder why our lives feel turned upside down, when really it's just our path calling to us from the wild.

When we leave whitespace available—open spaces of unrushed time—we can slow down and fall deeper in love with our priorities. That's the joy of missing out. As I type this, the word *unrushed* is underlined in an angry slash of red on my computer because society says it really isn't a word. We have a thousand words for *busy* but no single word for the true opposite—at least not a positive one. There isn't an English word for slowing down and savoring time. Isn't that ironic?

About a week after that incident, when I learned I was Jack's mom rather than his mommy, I was rushing into the store with Kate trailing behind. I was hurrying and walking too fast, so she called out and reached out her hand for mine. There had been a time, if I'm being totally honest, when this would have exasperated me because it slowed me down. I had to tamp that feeling down for a split second to realize, *This could be the last time she reaches for my hand.* And so I slowed down my pace, took her hand in mine, and lived in the moment. And I hope you will too. Be present for your tasks and events, give space for the people you love, and take good care of yourself.

Let's stop running around being busy and create some whitespace so we can slow down to enjoy life. I know this chapter has been filled with some tough love, but know that is what it is—love. I want you to have that space you need. You deserve that space, and I want to dive right to the heart of how to do that in our next chapter.

CHAPTER 11

HARMONIZE YOUR YES

Do your thing and don't care if they like it.
TINA FEY

To create the whitespace we need in our lives, we need to carve out that space for ourselves. We know we can't just make more time; we have to find it somewhere in our schedule. But how can we do that when our schedule is already packed full?

The seemingly obvious answer is that we need to say no more often. Simple advice, but it's not really that easy. Is it? Sometimes it may not feel so clean-cut because the one-size-fits-all answer of "no" fits about as well as a one-size-fits-all shirt—not very well at all.

Life is never one-size-fits-all. The challenge in life is not just saying no; it's the art of learning when your answer should be a "no" and when it should be a "yes." It's about finding *your* yes.

My favorite yes happened the spring after I opened the doors to inkWELL Press. A mere six months before, I fretted and worried about our launch. I told people jokingly that we would either be really happy after our launch or living in our car under a bridge. I smiled when I said it, but I didn't really think it was funny—it had a thin edge of truth behind it.

During that time we had financially tightened our belts, scraping together all our pennies to get the business off the ground. There were no social outings, no after-school activities. We were down to one car—a gray minivan with a long scratch down its side that had racked up about one hundred thousand miles. When launch day came with a flood of orders, it came, too, with a flood of relief.

I vividly remember the exact moment of my favorite yes. I was standing outside at a workshop when my phone rang. My husband is a man of few words, but as I pressed the phone to my ear, I heard a rush of excited words: There was a car . . . it had just become available . . . not just a car—*the car*. The car he had been dreaming of for years—a white Volkswagen GTI with manual shift. He sounded like a kid at Christmas sitting on Santa's lap. "What do you think?" he asked.

This man, who offered to follow me wherever my path might lead, who had supported and encouraged me to create my North Star, wanted to know if he could get his dream car. Without hesitation, I said *yes*.

The feeling of that yes washed over me. It felt so good, I don't think I could wipe that smile off my face if I had to—that's what *your* yes should feel like too.

If we believe the story *I just don't have enough time to focus on priorities*, it becomes a self-fulfilling prophecy. We need to start by clearing out the clutter so we can open up spaces for our yeses. The best way for us to do that is to uncommit.

IT'S TIME TO UNCOMMIT

That word *uncommit* may feel a little bit like a rock in your shoe. It's uncomfortable because we worry this means we are letting others down. I understand, because you are just like me—a giver. We givers always want to gift ourselves to others, and we never want anyone to feel that we've disappointed them.

But what if I told you this—you are already saying no all the time.

You see, every time you say yes, you are saying no to something else. Every. Single. Time. When we commit our time to others' priorities, it's at the expense of our own.

We say yes to volunteering on a committee we don't love, so we say no to time with family. We say yes to organizing an event for someone, so we say no to our personal goals. We say yes to coordinating a project for a group, so we say no to our own passion project. We cannot say yes without saying no. We have to steal the time, the energy, and the focus away from somewhere—we often just don't realize it.

It feels easy to say yes, to add "one more thing" to our day. One-more-thing-itis is real. We feel compelled to pile on one more thing, and another thing, and one more. Our schedule ends up looking like a plate of food at the end of the buffet line—heaping and overflowing—with no room left for what we really want . . . dessert. Just because you have the time doesn't mean you should say yes. We have to save room for our yeses, just like we have to save room for that dessert.

We feel obligated, though, to say yes because *have to* and *want to* have become indistinguishable—the lines are blurred. There is a big difference between happily giving our time to others and making ourselves do these things because we feel cornered. Here's a surprising truth: *saying no is not selfish; it's an opportunity to be selfless.*

Often the promise of doing #allthethings is just a cleverly disguised way to avoid facing trade-offs, which results in you scattering your focus and spending time on everything except the important things that actually matter. Opportunities seem innocent enough, but we forget the commitments that come with them: time, energy, focus. Our three most precious commodities.

———

With her piercing blue eyes, Katie exudes confidence. She is an inspiring entrepreneur with whip-smart advice on helping others grow their business while juggling her family of six.

EVERY TIME
YOU SAY

yes

YOU ARE
SAYING NO

TO SOMETHING ELSE

In 2016, though, Katie was overwhelmed. At the time, she was running a successful retail business with wholesale offerings, she was traveling extensively to speak at numerous events, she was teaching online classes for CreativeLive, *and* she gave birth to her fourth child. She told me, "I got to the end of the year and my business was succeeding, but I was exhausted. My family was exhausted. I was running myself ragged." Katie's plate wasn't just full; it was spilling over.

How could she possibly say no, though, to those opportunities when all those things were propelling her business? Most people would have seen no choices there, but Katie decided to give herself some space to think. She gave herself a one-day retreat, and in that whitespace she made some big decisions. She would stop traveling to speak, and she would stop selling retail and focus on licensing. Less travel, less scattered focus, with more concentration on family and key clients.

With less visibility, she wondered, *Will it affect revenue or impact business in a negative way?* But she never regretted it. She shared, "It reminded me I'm in control of how I spend my time and the expectations I set for myself. I have the freedom and flexibility to say yes or no, and I need to leverage that more. I have the power."

Was the change scary? Without question. Was there some doubt? Certainly. Did the relief feel huge? Absolutely.

Katie still had an obligation, though, to continue to move the business forward. Her family depends on her income, and, quite frankly, Katie enjoys her work tremendously. Quitting altogether wasn't an option. She had to employ some Squirrel Strategy.

She asked herself: If she wasn't going to travel, what could she do to keep her company visible? Starting her own podcast was the ideal solution. Instead of accepting in-person speaking events, she chose online summits or interviews on other people's podcasts and blogs. She got pickier about what she accepted and she discovered, "When I said yes to fewer things, I was able to give so much more of me. I do a better job, I get excited about the things I'm choosing to do, and I feel more passionate." Katie's business thrived, and with her newfound focus, she did too.

When Katie and I talked, she made the statement, "I worried people would forget me." And then she quickly followed up by apologizing and telling me it sounded vain. But I don't think it's vain at all. I know Katie personally, and she is not self-absorbed. She is generous and kind; she is thoughtful and patient with her children even though she constantly worries she is not. She is a giver, not a taker.

Here's some unfiltered truth, though—we all want to be seen. We all want to be acknowledged. We falsely believe we have to be everywhere in order to be seen. I think we all worry about being forgotten. We all want to make our mark on this world.

Success and the illusion of doing it all helps us feel like we are being seen. In reality, though, it can leave us feeling stretched too thin and pulled in far too many directions to make the impact we really want.

It's not just about uncommitting and saying no. You need to commit to what *is* important to you. Make a commitment with your schedule—it's an opportunity for you to pour more of your time, energy, and focus into the causes, people, and issues that truly matter to you.

Committing to nothing means you're distracted by everything. Commit to things that are important to you (and get rid of what isn't). Let's make our time more meaningful by "burning those boats" and making the biggest impact. Just as I discussed in chapter 4, it's the focus of energy that brings our greatest rewards.

We feel, though, as if we cannot quit. We all know winners never quit, and we want to feel like winners. Even when something is a losing proposition, we continue to invest more of our time. We fear failing and looking foolish. We hate to admit we made a mistake. Quitting feels like failure, but *quitting is not an end—it's the first step to redefining and refocusing your life*. Have the courage and confidence to cut out what's not working and make room for more of the yeses that belong to you.

YES TO REDISCOVERING YOU

If you are struggling with what your yes might look like, you are not alone. We sometimes lose ourselves in the roles we play. We might have to look hard to remind ourselves who we were before we had kids or before work got so intense or before tragedy struck our lives.

We have to find ourselves. Just because you feel lost doesn't mean you can't be found again.

Jenn rediscovered herself after her marriage of fifteen years crumbled. Her relationship had been filled with hardship, but it still hurt when her husband asked for a divorce. They had separated a few times in the past, but this time was different somehow—she knew it was the end of her marriage.

For the majority of their time together, Jenn had focused her energy on the constant restoration and work of her relationship. And in fighting hard for her marriage, she stifled her own identity in order to appease and smooth out the rough edges. For over a decade she told herself stories:

If I had been "enough," my marriage wouldn't be failing.
If I wasn't "too much," he would be happier.

Over the years, Jenn had adapted herself to fit who she believed she should be. She admitted, "I lived a very controlled life because I was trying to be something somebody else needed me to be."

While the divorce was hard, she chose to use it as an opportunity to heal and rewrite her stories. She needed to rediscover who she was without overthinking. She decided, "I'm just going to push this door wide open and let the pieces of myself become restored."

Jenn dedicated herself to what she termed "Jenn's Year of Yes." The rules were simple—as long as it fit within her values and wasn't dangerous, she would say yes to new opportunities for twelve months. Yes to little things, like an invitation to a New Year's Eve party were she knew no one, and yes to big things, like a last-minute trip to India. She said yes to flying out to help a friend set up her business, she said yes to living on a bus for two weeks supporting another friend's book release, and she said yes to traveling to Israel.

She showed up. She showed up for friends. She showed up for her community. She showed up for herself. She told me, "Each time I said yes, it just kept opening a door for me to heal, and something pivotal would happen. It allowed me to get out of my own way and find the path back to my authentic self."

Jenn said yes to opportunities she normally would have talked herself out of—like an out-of-state blind date set up by friends. A blind date that turned into a second date that stretched into a third.

Jenn shared, "None of it was random. For the first time in a long time, I was operating in my gifts. I am brave by nature; I just had lost my way. My season of saying yes helped me find my way back to myself." She now feels reenergized and more in tune with who she is at her core. Happily remarried to her blind date, Jenn is following her calling to help others live out their true selves. Her year of yes helped bring her full circle back to herself.

Sometimes *yes* is the very best word.

FINDING YOUR YES

The right yes we feel immediately—it feels great, like the wind at your back. Finding the right no isn't always so easy. We have to learn to filter and choose our yeses carefully.

You can't ask your mother or your best friend. You can't email me and ask me what list of activities you should do—it's not my yes; it's yours. Everyone's yes is different because, at its heart, it's tied to your North Star. You have to discover it for yourself.

I created a blueprint called Finding Your Yes that I use when I'm struggling to decide on an opportunity. I've shared it on the following page, but let me guide you through it. You start by writing out the opportunity. It's important to actually physically write it down because this is your very first chance to make your decision. When you take the time to write it out, how does it make you feel? Pay attention to your gut reaction.

Ask yourself, *Did I feel excited or nervous? Did I feel stress or dread?* If your feelings are negative, that's probably a quick no. It's important to point out, though, that feeling scared isn't necessarily a negative feeling. Fear can be an automatic reaction to big opportunities, so don't dismiss it right away as a negative feeling if nervousness strikes. Move on to the next step and dive a little deeper into the opportunity.

The next step is to write out why you want to take on this opportunity. As always, we want to begin with our foundation of why. *Why* do you want to do this? Taking a minute to analyze why you possibly want to accept this chance can help you see if it's aligned with your North Star. If it's not aligned or if you can't say strongly why you want to do it, this is an easy no.

What I love about this step is that there have been way too many times that I've gone through this exercise only to feel stumped by this question of why. Several times, without really thinking, I've watched my hand write out the words "I don't want to do this" or "I feel guilty" in this space. When I see my own words written there, it's the splash of cold water I need, and I immediately know I need to pass.

If, on the other hand, this opportunity feels in line with our North Star, then we need to look at our time next. Did you notice we didn't discuss time at all until after we decided *why* we wanted to do this? Too often we make choices based solely on time, and while time is a factor, it's not the ultimate decision maker. There are times when we hide behind our packed schedule as an excuse not to try new things or explore big opportunities. We want to use our North Star as our main guide for making our decisions—not time.

We need to estimate how much time the opportunity will take, and we need to be honest about the time commitment. If we are unsure, it's best to pad it a bit. It's better to overestimate so you can decide if you truly have the time to commit. If you do, that's great. There's really just one last question: If you say yes to this opportunity, what are you saying no to?

Even if we have the time, even if it's aligned with our North Star, every time we say yes, we say no to something else. Every single time. Decide how that feels, and if it feels right . . . congratulations, this is your yes!

If you don't have the time but you think you want to do it anyway,

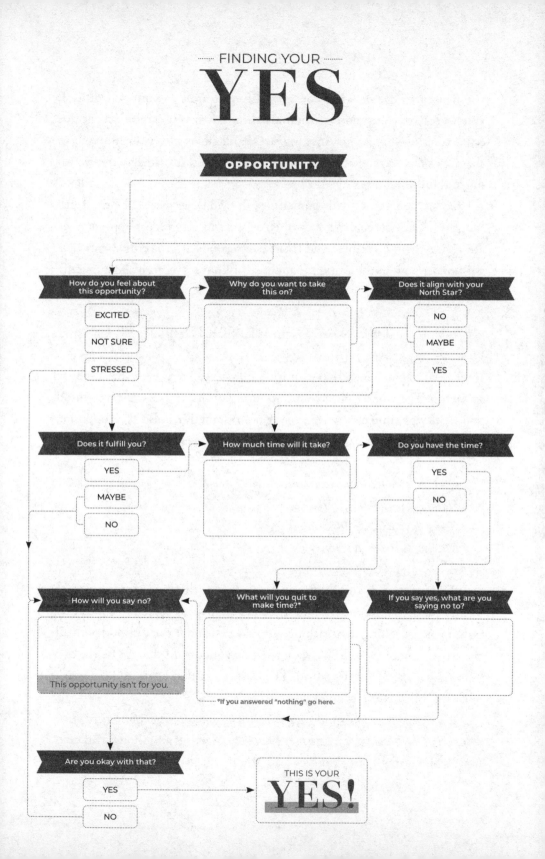

you'll need to decide what you are willing to quit in your schedule. If you don't have time and can't quit anything, then you cannot accept this opportunity—you are just inviting stress and chaos into your life. Accept that it's okay to say no, especially if your days are already filled with rewarding and fulfilling tasks.

Saying no can be hard. Sometimes the word *yes* just slips out of our mouths because it feels so good to see others smile and feel happy that we are giving them our time. And then, five seconds after it crosses our lips, we wonder how in the world it happened. I know, I've been there myself.

THE ART OF THE SOLID NO

If we need to pass on an opportunity, we first need to accept that it's okay to say no. The world will not stop spinning on its axis. I want to remind you that every time we say yes, we say no to something else. The opposite, then, also holds true. When we say no, we are, in effect, saying yes to:

Quality time with our loved ones
Having a reasonable workload
Being in control of our schedules
Making ourselves a priority

We need to stop and think about this the next time we are tempted to let the word *yes* slip out without a second thought. People are constantly pulling on us, calling to us, asking us to say yes, and it can get loud with all the requests for our time. We want the voice of our priorities to be the one rising above the din of the crowd. That's the voice that helps us distinguish what we truly believe is important.

We have to stop apologizing for prioritizing our priorities, for putting first things first, because that's where they belong. Being kind and thoughtful does not mean putting your priorities last. You can be kind but strong in your resolutions. For many of us, it's almost second nature to apologize when we have to tell someone we cannot volunteer, take on another responsibility, or step up for another committee.

We have to separate the request from the relationship. We often forget that saying no to a request is not a rejection of the person. Lysa TerKeurst wrote, "We must not confuse the command to love with the disease to please." I love that phrase—*the disease to please*—because it's true. We're saying yes to everyone to help ensure their happiness. We place ourselves at the bottom of our people-pleasing list.

Find the courage and compassion to communicate your no in a thoughtful way. But keep in mind, the answer is still no.

We've all heard the phrase "no is a complete sentence," and while I agree with the concept, I know it's not easy to implement in real life. Most of us don't feel comfortable with just saying no, so we end up overexplaining, overapologizing, and sometimes getting suckered into saying yes after all! The key is to make saying no easier for yourself so you are more confident saying it.

My favorite technique to accomplish this is a simple but effective method called the Sandwich Strategy. Imagine a standard, everyday sandwich: two pieces of bread with some kind of filling nestled in the middle. When we need to say no to an opportunity, the no is the meat of our message, so we simply sandwich it in between two slices of kindness. Here's how you can use the Sandwich Strategy to say no to a request for a committee:

SANDWICH STRATEGY: I am so flattered you thought of me for this important committee. Unfortunately, I have several other activities I've committed to, so I'm unable to give it the time it deserves. I am thrilled, though, that you are pulling together a group of people for such a worthwhile cause!

Do you see the clear no right there in the middle? But because it's started and finished with compassion, it's easier to swallow. And, bonus for us, it's easier to give.

DON'T GET CAUGHT OFF GUARD

Many times we say yes because we are taken off guard—we are asked in passing in the hallway at work, while we are cheering on our kids at a soccer game, or at some other time when we are not prepared, so we default to saying yes.

The trick is to have a go-to phrase ready. When someone asks us, "What do you have going on this weekend?" it's easy to shrug our shoulders and tell them we are free. Then, when they ask us to man the dunking booth at the school carnival for three hours, we can't say no. Instead, when asked about our plans, we can reply, "I am not sure. I'll have to check my calendar. Why?"

Let them tell you about the opportunity before giving carte blanche to your calendar. You need to entertain the opportunity before you make a decision. Remember, time is a factor, but it's not the deciding factor.

There are times, too, when you'll need to work through that Finding Your Yes blueprint to decide. Give yourself some space to weigh out whether it's your yes or not. Often we default to saying *maybe* or *probably*, which are soft yeses that we then feel obligated to follow through on.

Let the person requesting your time know you are seriously considering it, but it's not a soft yes:

SANDWICH STRATEGY: That sounds like something I'd normally be interested in. I'm not sure I'll be able to give it the time it deserves, so I need some time to think about it. I'll let you know Friday. I really appreciate you thinking of me.

By the way, have you noticed I use the phrase "the time it deserves" in both these examples? I love that term because I'm not blaming it on being busy, and I'm not elevating myself. I'm using this as a chance to show the person I understand their project/task/committee is important to them. I am acknowledging them and that this opportunity is significant to them. (But that doesn't mean it's necessarily important to me.)

It's also key to lay out your own set of ground rules—your boundaries for how many opportunities you want to allow. Decide for yourself: How many nights a week are you willing to block off time to commit to doing things outside your house? How many days a week are you willing to do something that isn't tied to your North Star? Decide this for yourself, and then you need to stick to it.

SANDWICH STRATEGY: Thanks so much for the invite to movie night! I'm sorry to miss, but I'm trying to spend more evenings at home during the week. I've heard it's a good movie, though, so I'm sure you'll have a great time.

I recently spoke at an event and shared the Sandwich Strategy. One woman in the crowd started to raise her hand, put it back down, and then timidly raised it again. I could tell she was struggling with the idea of saying no and there was some sort of internal battle going on in her head, so I asked her if I could help.

"But what if it's Sunday school you want to say no to?" she asked incredulously. "I teach Sunday school each week, and I really don't enjoy it." She looked embarrassed to admit this aloud, and even though I know she is not alone in feeling this way, I understood it took courage to say these words to a room full of people. I pushed a little bit for more information, and she admitted, "I love my church, I love my kids, but I don't love teaching other kids. I want to help, but teaching on Sundays is making me dread attending."

You might have noticed the same thing I did in her statement: she was having a hard time separating the request from the relationship. She felt she could not let her church down, so she believed she had no choice but to keep slogging through her Sunday mornings. Now I don't know about you, but I believe most churches want people to be excited about Sundays—not dread them. Because she does want to volunteer, it's not a hard no but more of a softer no:

> **SANDWICH STRATEGY:** I really love volunteering for our church
> and helping it grow. I don't believe, though, that the children's minis-
> try is the best fit for me. I want to make sure the kids are excited about
> Sunday school, and I don't think I'm the right person to help do that for
> them. I want to give back and make sure my gifts are used in the best
> way possible for our congregation. Where else can I best help?

She smiled brightly at me when I gave this suggestion and shared that she was excited to find the right place for herself at her church. I could tell it was a relief to think about saying no to Sunday school all while still giving back.

Maybe you're in a similar situation at your kids' school, your charitable group, or even your work. I understand there are times when you feel you cannot say no, but I promise you can. And you can do it in ways that are respectful and kind. Yes, even if it is your boss who needs to be told no.

Listen. Bosses and managers—they are human just like you and me. They forget how much is piled on our plates because they are too busy looking at their own. When they add more to our workload, they may not realize we are already stretched thin with a thousand other projects they assigned in the past. It's our job to stake our boundaries and remind them.

We need our bosses and managers to clearly communicate what they believe are the priorities in our workload:

> **SANDWICH STRATEGY:** I am happy to work on this project. I am also working on X, Y, and Z, so which of these should I take off my plate so I can work on this project to the best of my ability? I want to make sure to give it the time it deserves.

Deliver your sandwich with positivity, calmness, and the best results you can.

I'm not going to pretend saying no is easy, but when you say no, you open up opportunities for even bigger yeses. All those nos I had to give when I was preparing my business to launch? Those resulted in a business I love—and it allowed me to say that big, beautiful yes to my husband when he called me about his dream car.

I want to encourage you to say no to mindlessly scrolling and say yes to walks together as a family after dinner, to say no to TV binge-watching and yes to actual phone calls with friends, to say no to opportunities that don't fulfill you and yes to your passion project. It's time for you to go out to dinner with friends, to try that yoga class you've been dying to try for months. It's time to find that harmony you crave—the joy of missing out.

 ## LET ME HELP

Let me help you sort through the noise to find your ideal yes. I want to give you your own copy of the Finding Your Yes blueprint that you can print again and again when making decisions about opportunities. Get free access to this bonus feature at joyofmissingout.com/chapter11.

CHAPTER 12

HARMONIZE LIFE

You may not control all the events that happen to you,
but you can decide not to be reduced by them.

MAYA ANGELOU

Lunch was about to be served, and I watched hungrily as the waiters passed by with heaping plates of steaming food. As one waiter swiftly skirted around our table, I caught the eye of my friend sitting across from me. I smiled, embarrassed she had caught me stalking the food, but she didn't smile back. She opened her mouth to say something and quickly closed it back up as if she was afraid the words would fall out of her mouth and onto the table in front of us.

I noticed her eyes well up with tears, and then she let forth a string of words so fast, I almost didn't catch them, "IhatetotellyoubutIampregnant." *Pregnant?! Really?!* I'm not sure which one stung me first, the realization that she was the fifth friend to share the same announcement that month or the bitter understanding that I had become the person everyone wanted to avoid with their good news.

I contorted my face to force a fake smile and told her not to be sorry, that it was cause for celebration. And then, with that stupid smile plastered on my face, I quickly excused myself to go to the bathroom where I cried the ugliest cry you've ever seen—complete with hiccups and a runny nose. One woman opened the door to come in, took one look at me, and hightailed it out of there. She was not about to walk in on that hot mess.

I splashed cold water on my face to minimize the damage and headed out to face my friend. Thank goodness for the stack of shoestring fries waiting for me at the table to help me hide my salty cheeks.

I was happy for her—I really was. But I'm going to be honest with you, I also felt sucker punched. How was it possible that everywhere I looked *everyone* was pregnant? At that moment, I had nine friends at various stages of pregnancy, and I think every celebrity to grace the pages of a magazine was sporting a giant beach ball for a belly. I couldn't seem to get away from the fact that everyone was pregnant. Everyone but me.

THE WORLD IS NOT AGAINST YOU

It's hard not to wallow when you think you're getting cheated. When it seems like everyone else has what you want without even trying—getting married, receiving a promotion at work, or running a thriving business. It can feel like you are the only one in the whole wide world not finding success.

The good news is that it's not really true. Everyone wasn't pregnant; it was just my perception. Technically it's called frequency illusion, which is the phenomenon where an idea or concept you've been thinking about suddenly seems to pop up everywhere even though you never noticed it before. You might have experienced this when shopping for a new car. Suddenly that brand of car is next to you at the light and turning in front of you and parked across the street. When it's a car, it can feel like a funny coincidence, but when it's something big, like trying to get pregnant, it can feel like the universe is playing a mean joke on you.

Our brain can overlook countless items in our surroundings, but once our brain takes notice of something it considers significant (in my case, pregnant women), it starts to pull those occurrences out of the background noise. Because of our selective attention, it feels as if they are appearing again and again in our world. Really, the truth is, those things were there all along; we just didn't take notice. It's our mindset kicking in.

We started this book together talking about mindset and here we've come full circle. Because that, my friend, is at the heart of productivity—especially in the terms we talk about it. When you work to live with priority and you create an intentional life for yourself, 90 percent of it is the lens you use to view the world. Your brain scans and categorizes all those millions of bits of information it's inundated with every second. It comes down to choices.

Now I know changing your life circumstances isn't always possible. Sometimes all you can change is your perception or opinion about the situation. The bottom line is, *you can't control reality, but you can control how you react and respond to it.* Tough times and hardships are inevitable in everyone's lives, but how we view what we're going through is completely up to us.

———

Elaina* is one of those women who was simply born to be a mom. When her father died, she willingly placed her own childhood on hold and stepped in to take care of her younger siblings. When it was time to have her own children, Elaina felt she was ready—she was excited to be the perfect mom. She read every book and did her very best to do everything just right.

Her son, Davis, is an extraordinarily bright and creative child. When it came to school, though, he just couldn't seem to stay out of trouble. *Won't apply himself . . . can't sit still . . . disruptive. . . .* At every teacher conference, Elaina heard these words thrown out again and again, each one feeling like a sharp slap across her cheek.

Elaina began to wonder, "*Why me?* I looked around at all the other

———

* Name has been changed.

moms proudly comparing their success stories on the playground, and I felt inadequate. Why had this happened to me? I did everything I could to be the best mom. Why wasn't I doing better?"

Elaina decided she needed to change the way she felt about parenting. She had always longed to be a mother, and she was tired of feeling like it was a chore. The constant questioning of herself was exhausting, so Elaina chose to give herself some space to readjust her mindset.

She didn't know what that would look like, but she knew she needed a change. She used her daily commute to allow herself space to think and simply open up her heart to understanding her situation. Morning after morning she got in her car and searched for clarity. Early one day, while sitting at a stoplight, it hit her: her situation wasn't a punishment. She realized Davis didn't happen to her; *she* happened to Davis. She was a gift given to him—he was lucky to have a mom who wasn't willing to give up on him.

Since coming to this epiphany, Elaina has felt stronger as a parent and has looked at her role as Davis's advocate in a completely different light. She's come to realize that it's not about being the perfect parent—it's about being the best parent she can be *for Davis.*

You see, *we get caught up in asking if our glass is half full or half empty—we forget that sometimes it's not even our glass at all.* Some of the events and trials and tribulations we experience aren't about us at all. When we can grasp that, it can change our perception of how life is treating us.

We need to focus on what we can control, including our emotions, desires, judgments, creativity, determination, and, of course, mindsets. This allows us to grow beyond the things we can't control and change our attitudes toward them instead.

We have to stop getting caught up in the pointless things in life we can't control—including what others think of us, or what they say when we say no or when we prioritize. It's easy to get caught up in others' opinions of us, to mold ourselves to fit their tight constraints of what it means to be "right" even at the expense of ourselves.

Actress Viola Davis knows a thing or two about creating your own mindset when life seems to be against you. Growing up with an abusive alcoholic father, she would wake up some mornings unsure if she would have food to eat, but she didn't let that keep her down. She shared, "They tell you to develop a thick skin so things don't get to you. What they don't tell you is that your thick skin will keep everything from getting out, too. Love, intimacy, vulnerability. I don't want that. Thick skin doesn't work anymore. I want to be transparent and translucent. For that to work, I won't own other people's shortcomings and criticisms. I won't put what you say about me on my load."

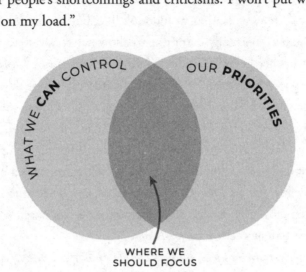

WHAT WE **CAN** CONTROL

OUR **PRIORITIES**

WHERE WE
SHOULD FOCUS

Viola is right. There's no need to accept the burden of others' criticisms. When we keep our focus in the sweet spot of what we can control and our priorities, we can live happier. I'm not going to lie to you and tell you that standing strong and sticking to your priorities is always easy, but I can promise you it will be worth it. It will take sacrifice—we have to stop trying to do it all.

The girl in the cape isn't me—and I don't want her to be. I have no interest in being Superwoman, but there are times where I feel compelled to try. Even worse, I sometimes feel others trying to clip that cape on my shoulders, and I start to feel the weight of it dragging me down. You have probably felt that too.

Ultimately, though, it's your life, and it's up to you to choose how you live it.

YOUR FUTURE IS YOURS TO WRITE

When we get caught up in focusing on what we are "supposed" to do, we just keep going through the motions of life rather than doing what we really want to do. We assure ourselves that someday this cycle will stop, that once certain conditions get better, everything will improve.

We tell ourselves these stories:

I need to work weekends until I make partner, then I'll have time to spend with my family.
I have so much to do. I just don't have the luxury of going out with my friends.
Someday things will be easier and I'll get to do the things I really want.

Unfortunately, "someday" is like a mirage on the horizon; each time we get closer, it keeps moving farther and farther away. Truly, without effort on our part, nothing will change and our priorities will continue to be put last.

If we wait until all of our tasks are done to sit down and enjoy what's most important, that time will never come—there's always some sort of urgent work to be done. When we don't take the time to actively choose how we spend our days, each task on our list feels urgent and unavoidable. It feels justifiable to postpone date night with our spouse, miss a movie with friends, or skip the gym (again). We end up putting it off, exhausted at the end of our day and too tired to enjoy the things we, in our heart of hearts, truly enjoy most. That's not the way we want to live.

Stop borrowing from today to make tomorrow great. Instead, let's choose to make the most of today, knowing that when we spend our days focusing on priorities, we are investing in our future.

———

I met Savannah recently on a trip and was instantly struck by how much she embodies this idea of taking time for herself in order to invest in her future. Upon first meeting her and hearing her speak with a true excitement for life, it seemed like she's got her life all figured out. But like many of us, her path has been filled with stones and rocks.

A competitive gymnast throughout her childhood, Savannah happily grew up spending long days at the gym. Her parents' divorce when she was fourteen, though, meant she suddenly had to quit the team. Losing this sense of identity caused her to compensate by partying too much. She felt lost.

She knew, though, that there was something out there for her—she just wasn't sure what it was. On her eighteenth birthday, she bought herself a one-way ticket to the Virgin Islands. She knew no one there and had no idea what she would do when she arrived, but as the wheels of her plane hit the ground, she vowed to stop partying so she could find clarity in her life.

Savannah started with the one thing she knew she loved—being active outdoors. She headed to a water sports shop and offered to work for free in exchange for knowledge. Seven days a week she arrived before the sun rose to rake the beaches and begin her work, and in return she received training on teaching paddleboarding, sailing, and windsurfing. Each day as the sun set, she left work to head to her second job at a restaurant so she could cover her rent.

Three years later she was running her own catamaran charter focused on healthy eating and yoga—passions rediscovered from her former life as a gymnast. She found harmony in her newfound life, but even when a person finds harmony, it isn't always smooth sailing.

In 2017 hurricanes hit the Caribbean, causing mass destruction. Savannah could have, again, lost her identity, but she looked at this disaster as a new opportunity—a chance to explore. She mused, "While I love the crystal-clear waters of the beaches, it does limit me from seeing the mountains and rivers."

The idea of river guiding had appealed to her for some time, but it had always coincided with her charter season—it was always just out of reach. As she explained, though, "The hurricane opened up a new opportunity, and I thought to myself, *This is my time.*" Most people would find that a hard choice to make—seeing a hurricane as an opportunity—but that's what Savannah did.

She chose to head to the mountains of Colorado and, through guiding, discovered "the way a river moves is a very different dance than the ocean." With her new knowledge, Savannah now plans to drop anchor in exotic ports around the world where she'll charter her catamaran half the year and then run river expeditions during the other half, exploring different parts of the world in a unique way.

She shared with me, "If I spent all my time in the mountains, I would miss diving with sea turtles, but if I only swam the warm waters of the Caribbean, I'd never get to see the sun set on the mountains." Savannah has taken her passions and made them into one beautiful, harmonious life for herself—one that is no longer out of reach.

Just as Savannah scans the horizon searching for rocks and waves in the water to help her guide her boats, she is now looking forward to her future and navigating herself toward the life she really wants. She is actively making choices to create that future for herself.

You may have noticed in many of the examples I've shared that some of the women didn't know at the start exactly what the future held. They just knew there was something better out there, and they opened themselves up to the possibilities.

This joy-of-missing-out journey will sometimes lead us outside our comfort zones. And that's a good thing. Our comfort zone is a dangerous place to live long term because as much as we seem to enjoy comfort, we are often happiest when challenged and making progress toward our North Star.

We love our checklists, but this space outside our comfort zone doesn't always have them—and that makes it hard to feel confident in what we are doing. The growth is difficult and can be filled with doubt. There will be times where the critic inside our heads will make us question everything—maybe even blame us for the disruption we've been feeling.

When we begin to intentionally invest our time, energy, and focus on important things today, we end up with a more abundant life and more accomplishments in the future. We feel good about what we've gotten done. I use that term *invest* here very purposefully because that is what we are doing with our most precious commodities. Let's invest them in things that matter to us.

Remember those 72 hours we discovered back in chapter 10? Those 72 hours we have left after work and sleep have been accounted for? Let's look at those 72 hours a different way; let's look at them as money we have to invest. If you had $72 to spend for your week, would you start handing out five-dollar bills to anyone who asked? Or would you budget your money and make sure you took care of the important items like food, rent, and your bills? We think nothing, though, of handing out our time to anyone and everyone who asks. We wouldn't invest our money on things without some sort of return on investment, and yet we are quick to give away our time.

The return we are looking for with our time is generally stronger relationships, better health, or reaching our goals. We need to spend our time like we do our money, on the things that matter most—our priorities.

I can imagine the critics rolling their eyes and reminding me there is no time to invest—our schedules are already so full! I hear you. Let's get back to our idea of thinking of time as money, because I think that will help bring this idea home.

Most of us have a limited amount of funds in our bank accounts—just as we have a limited amount of time we can spend. What happens, though, when our car breaks down? Do we just say to ourselves, *Oh, well. There's no money to fix the car, so I guess I can't go to work*? No, we somehow find the money to pay for it because it's a priority. We tighten our belts a bit, we stop getting our Frappuccino from the coffee shop, we skip the highlights in our hair, we cut back on the sushi dinners. We focus our money on the priority and save in places that aren't as high on our priority list. Time works exactly the same way. We need to cut out the less important things that are pulling us in a million directions and instead focus on our priorities.

This is why the discovery process I talked about in section 1 is our foundation. It's so important to know what direction we want to go. That helps us see where we want to invest our time. Productivity is *not* doing lots of stuff fast. It is purposefully and consistently moving in one direction. The direction *we* want to go.

Try taking one step in four different directions. Where did you end up? Not very far from where you started. Now take four steps in one direction. Where did you end up this time? You moved ahead, didn't you? That's the momentum we need. Newton's law of inertia states that an object at rest stays at rest and an object in motion stays in motion with the same speed and in the same direction unless acted upon by an unbalanced force. You see, productivity = velocity. You just need to get started moving in the one direction you desire—toward your North Star.

DON'T APOLOGIZE FOR BEING YOU

I want to challenge you to make some tough choices. Choose to rethink what it means to be busy, choose how you spend your time, and choose how you treat your priorities. After all, if they are priorities, shouldn't they be treated as priorities? They should sit front and center when you plan out your day each morning. We can allow others to take control of our calendars and our time with their own priorities and urgent tasks, or we can be in charge.

We have to keep in mind that the joy of missing out is all about harmony—not balance. We use counterbalance so we can lean into our priorities for a time in order to move in the direction we want. I have created what I call Quarterly Crusades. Each quarter I choose a top priority and focus on it. You might be working toward a promotion at work, hitting a personal fitness goal, or actively creating time for a passion project. It doesn't matter what it is; what matters is that it's important to you.

Every three months we need to sit down and decide what goals need to be set in order to move us forward in that area where we want to grow. We have to resolve that, for the next ninety days, we are focusing on this area. And then we need to plan. Using our priority list and the five Ps I talked about in chapter 9, we make sure this focused area is the first thing we schedule into our day.

We have to let go of other projects that are potential distractions to our success. In our desire to do everything, we scatter our attention in a thousand directions. We want to focus.

Now don't get me wrong. Don't be misguided and think this is permission to neglect all the other areas of your life. That's not possible, and it's not healthy. Life will continue to run, but when we have the clarity to know the direction we are moving in, we can prioritize where we spend our time.

Let's go back to the bike analogy we used to describe counterbalance. When you turn a corner and lean into one side of your bike, do you let go of the handlebars? Do you stop pedaling? No. Everything continues to move, even while you shift your balance. Your hands hold on to the handlebars and your feet continue to push down on the pedals—they move automatically.

You see, this is where those systems we've discussed come into play. They allow life to continue moving, but they allow that to happen without you losing your focus. Nobody in the history of the universe ever accomplished great things by trying to do everything.

We find harmony when we counterbalance: we even out heavy workdays with lighter workdays, we fill our weekends with personal time instead of work, and we shift our mindset and remember life is not meant to be endured but enjoyed.

Part of finding this harmony, too, is forgiving yourself for mistakes you've made in your life. Maybe you have run your life like a circus and you are ready for it to stop. Maybe you have said yes far too often, or maybe you have spent so much time on other people's needs that you have forgotten who you are deep inside.

It's okay. It's not what you've done in the past that matters; it's what you do moving forward that counts. Failure is what you make of it. Failure is sometimes the road to long-term success.

One of my favorite illustrations of how failure can be transformative lies deep in the sandy ocean beds of Sri Lanka. The floor of the Indian

NOBODY

IN THE HISTORY OF THE

EVER ACCOMPLISHED

GREAT THINGS

— BY TRYING TO DO —

EVERYTHING

Ocean is scattered with the quiet remains of over two hundred shipwrecks that met tragic fates over the course of thousands of years. Each one could be deemed a failure—a failed journey—but something amazing happened as these ships settled into the deep.

These sunken vessels became part of the environment, and an abundance of marine life wrapped around them over time. They transformed from ghostly hulking ships into magnificent coral reefs teeming with life— fish, sponges, clams, squid, mollusks, and eels live and thrive among these lost ships.

There is a sad story behind every single wreck and its unfinished journeys, but from tragedy comes intense beauty. We need to have the same perspective about our own mistakes and failures, our stumbling blocks that have held us back in the past. Each one is an opportunity for growth, and yes, even for beauty.

This transformation to coral reefs did not happen overnight; it took time and patience before new life took hold. Your transition to living a life centered on priority will take time too. Time, patience, and energy are needed to start making the shift.

Know that change will not happen overnight and that sometimes victories are small, but take time to celebrate them and be encouraged that the life you want is out there. Give yourself grace to rediscover what makes you happy and be unapologetically you. Fall back in love with yourself and fill your world with people who support and love you. Spend your time in ways that feel like investments—invest in relationships and activities that fulfill you. Try to let go of what does not align with your priorities and the life you truly want to live.

What I want for you is more than a productive life: I want you to have the beautiful life you deserve. Now it's up to you to go get it.

LET'S START

I've saved my hardest story for last. Maybe I felt like I needed you to be really invested before I shared it, but more likely it's because the idea of telling this story scares me to my core. I want to share it with you because I know I've been asking you for a lot throughout this book. I've challenged you to work hard to change your mindset and to create a life centered on your priorities. And I realize this might feel incredibly difficult, especially if you have a past to overcome—a past that has let you down, that has disappointed you and made you feel like this life you are wanting is always just out of reach.

I've encouraged you to let go of old stories, and now it's time to let go of one of mine . . .

I bought my first home at the age of twenty-three. I was single and fresh out of my first year of teaching. My friends all thought I was crazy, but they also told me how amazing it was that I didn't wait to make my dream come true. They called me strong. And I liked it—because deep inside I knew I was not.

No one knew why I suddenly had the burning desire to buy a house. They didn't know I did it only to prove to myself that I could create a life of my own. They didn't know I was doing it because I was secretly running from myself. Truth be told, I had been running from my own shadow for years at that point.

Back in my sophomore year of college, I had moved into an apartment complex along with seven of my sorority sisters. We lived across the parking lot from one another, like a real-life version of *Friends*. We were constantly at each other's apartments having impromptu dinners or getting dressed together on Friday nights. I *loved* it.

Late one evening as I was getting out of the shower, I heard a noise on my porch. I knew my roommate was out for the night, so I peered outside and could just make out the outline of a man doing his very best to break into my apartment. I turned on the porch light, but that didn't seem to faze him at all. He rattled and shook the windows; he twisted and yanked on the doorknob.

I won't get into the details of how I ended up face-to-face with this tall psychopath on my front porch, but let it suffice for me to tell you that for three months I slept in my roommate's bed. She eventually insisted she was tired of me hogging the covers and made me move back into my own bedroom. Once I did, I went to bed with a baseball bat nestled on the pillow next to me. But I didn't sleep.

Eventually I learned to lessen the tight grip on my bat. Life moved on, but I continued to keep a vigilant watch as I walked to my car in a parking garage, and I was always overly guarded when I was alone in my apartment— every noise made me jump. When I went out with friends, I was incredibly cautious; I was almost always the designated driver because I didn't want to feel out of control in a room full of strangers. For years I couldn't be alone once the sun went down.

And then one night, one terrible night, I went out with a friend for dinner and dancing. That night was no different from any of the other nights I went out—I drank cokes rather than vodka—but somehow I found myself stumbling back home at 5:00 a.m. with mascara-stained cheeks, dazed and battered, with my shirt on backward and inside out.

I remember my fingers shaking as I tried to put the key into the lock, and then I tumbled into my bedroom, taking one look at myself in the mirror and turning away in disgust. My cheeks filled with a deep shame I didn't really deserve. I twisted the dial of my shower to scalding hot and scrubbed my body raw. Still wrapped in a towel with lobster-red skin, I angrily yanked my sheets off the bed and grabbed armfuls of my clothing from the closet, and threw them into the washer. Even though it wasn't my fault, I still felt a disgrace I wanted to scrub away. I was desperate for my world to feel clean again.

I told no one. No one at all. I did nothing but silently tear myself apart as if I were to blame for the darkness I was living through. And then one morning I woke up (I use the term "woke up" here ironically since I was, once again, no longer sleeping at night) and decided I wasn't going to live that life of being a victim again. I'd had enough of that in my past. I called a listing agent two days later and began the search for a house. I needed to prove to myself I would be okay being on my own.

And I did. I bought a house, I taught myself home repair, and I patched and painted my little home. Six months later John moved in next door, and my story of how I bought a tiny little house and married my next-door neighbor seemed magical, but it was always steeped, in my mind, in my secret.

I am telling you this story not because I want you to believe I am strong. I am telling you so that you can see that I felt weak. I was too afraid for a very long time to speak up.

We all have times in our lives when we feel like this. I feel certain that you, too, have had times when you felt like you were a victim, just like I did. Some of us have been victims of oppression, many of us have been victims of our situations, and lots of us are victims of our circumstances or upbringings.

But we all are survivors.

We can choose to see ourselves as we really want to be. We don't have to fake it until we make it. We can, as psychologist Amy Cuddy shared in her TED Talk, "fake it till [we] become it." I want to encourage you to remember that you are stronger/faster/smarter/better than you think. That, I can guarantee you.

Our lives are filled with highs and lows. For me, the valley I was in was low and deep, and there were times when I couldn't feel the warmth of the sun. There is a strength inside of us, though. Even when we feel weak, it's there deep inside.

We can take our experiences and allow them to swallow us whole, or we can use them as fuel to drive us, to push the boundaries of what we know and break beyond our comfort zones—to find the path our North Star is ready to light.

I've moved forward, but I haven't forgotten. There are still nights when John is gone and I lie awake, fearful of every noise in the dark. I continue to stay hypervigilant when walking by myself, and I'll never go to a grocery store alone at night. Not ever. These parts of me will never go away; they are woven into the fabric of me. But I have come to peace with that. I can choose to see these parts of myself as flaws, or I can see them as the scars I've acquired over my life. Scars that used to be raised, angry-red welts that now have faded into silvery trails, marking the path where I've been.

We all have scars, my friend.

What is holding you back from your fulfilling life? Is it fear? Is it the comfort and safety of what you already know? Yes, this book is about productivity, but at its heart, it's about the choices we make: the hard choices, the easy choices, the everyday choices. Our lives are defined by choices.

And now you need to make a choice. Do you want to stay on the path you are on, or do you want to make some changes to work toward the life you want?

Take one step forward, one tiny step, each and every day. Each step of this process builds upon the last, creating a strong framework for a fulfilling life. We began with a foundation of discovery that helps us clarify how we want to spend our time. This clarity in turn reveals how we need to integrate simplicity into our daily lives. And finally the simplicity allows us to live a life of harmony—a life of contentment because we are living true to ourselves. At the heart of each of these four sections we've been adjusting our beliefs, our boundaries, and our behaviors, all of which influence our lives and affect our productivity.

The red thread running through and anchoring each step is priority. It is possible to live a life centered on what matters most; happiness is possible when you make every day count. You just have to choose to begin.

Today is a good day to start.

LET ME HELP

Before you allow the back cover to close on this book, I have one last question for you: Did the messages of this book resonate with you?

Slow down and rethink busy.
Focus on priorities.
Live a life that feels meaningful to you.
Choose a life centered on your priorities.
Embrace the joy of missing out.

If they did . . . if you believe this life you have dreamed of in the past is now more within reach, let's spread this message. One of the most powerful ways to instill change in ourselves is by being accountable to others who are willing to support us.

I want to encourage you to pull together a group of friends and ask them to read this book so you can work through the questions together. Agree to meet often to go through the exercises and activities, to cheer one another on and pull one another up when you stumble (because there will be stumbles). Talk about what you agree with—and what you don't.

Strip aside the facades of the perfect life and share with one another. Be real and honest with one another—and yourselves.

We are much stronger together. Let's start this movement.

Tonya

WE CAN TAKE OUR EXPERIENCES
AND ALLOW THEM TO
SWALLOW US WHOLE

OR WE CAN USE THEM AS FUEL TO

ACKNOWLEDGMENTS

I have a confession to make. Anytime I think I might like a book, I first read the introduction and then flip immediately to the very back—to the acknowledgments. I want to know who the author is and why she wrote her book. I think that tells you a lot about a writer. You see, the acknowledgments reveals priorities—and if you ever want to understand your own, simply take the time to write your own acknowledgments.

I have to begin with you, John Dalton. Almost twenty years ago we ran away to Florence, Italy and said "I do." The morning of my wedding, I couldn't sleep, so I left my hotel room just before dawn to walk the quiet city streets and pray. I watched the old women sweeping the damp sidewalks and the men hauling baskets of bread, I watched the city wake up and reflected on how my life would change.

I didn't know it at the time, but you were a mere two minutes ahead of me doing the exact same thing. Unknowingly, we walked the exact same path that morning. We laughed about it afterwards, but I now know that it was just the first of many paths we would walk together. We first walked alone but now we walk side by side.

Thank you so much for walking with me and always holding my hand. You are the rock upon which I stand.

Jack and Kate, this book that you hold in your hands represents my biggest lifetime goal but you two are, by far, my proudest accomplishment. I could not do what I do without you. Your willingness to pitch in at home and at my office, your words of encouragement at night around the table, and your enthusiasm for the work we do as a family makes my heart feel like a butterfly caught in a net. I love you both.

Mom and Dad, you have always been unwavering in your belief that I can accomplish anything. I've always been in awe of the way you are able to give your time and effort to others—even when it seemed there was none to give. I am grateful for having you as a model for what you can give to others.

To the Herridge Family, I am forever grateful for your never-ending love of me and my family. I cannot put into words how lucky I feel to have you in our lives and how supported you made us all feel during our big leap.

I am incredibly thankful for my inkWELL Press team who have made it possible for me to accomplish so much more than I ever could on my own: Emma, Heather, Timara, Jordan, and Siobhan. I have endless amounts of love for each of you and how tirelessly you each work to allow our North Star to shine so brightly. Thank you for being a part of my vision and a part of my extended family.

To all of my friends and family, too countless to mention, thank you for believing in me and encouraging me. You have pushed me to the very best version of myself. I wish there was room here to personally thank each one of you. I do want to give a quick callout to just a few individuals that have influenced me as I wrote this book: Kim and Geoff Walls, Diann and Pete Bennett, the Osborn Family, the Holmsten Family, the Thompson/Prince Families, Jim Cali, Marshawn Daniels, Katie Hunt, Myrna Daramy, Jamie Larson, Lynn Penny, Jenn Jett Barrett, Kristen Ley, Lauren Dillard, Caroline Hull, Jordan Robbins, and my friend Emily Potts, who taught me that life is far too short and to live every minute fully.

I am grateful for the Yates & Yates team and especially to Mike Salisbury, who is more than just an agent. You promised me you would be my Sherpa and guide me through the process, but I've come out the other side with much more—a trusted friend. I am grateful for you.

Thank you to my entire Thomas Nelson team: Jenny, Jamie, Sara, Stephanie, Tim, Brigitta, Karin, Aryn, Shea, and everyone on the sales team who believed in me and the message of this book.

My Super Connector Media Team of Maggie, Angela, Chris, Chloe, Jen, and Chris. I truly believe God places people on a path at just the right time. I am grateful he placed you on mine. Brittney, you have been a big part of my team long before we were #TeamTonya. I have always felt grateful to have you by my side.

To the women who allowed me to share their stories in this book: When we shine a light on our own journey, it acts as a beacon for others. It allows them to know that while the path may be long and rocky, none of us are alone—we light the way for one another. Thank you for the willingness and the courage to share your light.

To my IWP family: the podcast listeners, the TonyaTV watchers, the planner-users, and those of you who connect with me in my Facebook group. Thank you for listening and for all the kind notes and emails you have sent my way. On days that are hard—and there are hard days for me, just as there are for you—those are the things I cling tightly to for my own momentum. So thank you, thank you, thank you.

And finally, to you, dear reader. Those early mornings when I rose to write this book, I imagined you sitting next to me, I pictured you listening to the audiobook in your car, and I saw you standing face-to-face with me taking in the words I had written. I thought of you in every step of this journey. This book has always been about you.

NOTES

JOMO

ix "emotionally intelligent antidote": Inspired by Kristen Fuller, "JOMO: The Joy of Missing Out," *Psychology Today*, July 26, 2018, https://www.psychologytoday.com/us/blog/happiness-is -state-mind/201807/jomo-the-joy-missing-out.

INTRODUCTION

xv "For me [busy] feels like": Posted in the author's private Facebook group, November 6, 2018.

CHAPTER 2: DISCOVER CHOICE

17 "Illogically, we reasoned": Greg McKeown, *Essentialism: The Disciplined Pursuit of Less* (New York: Crown Business, 2014), 16.

19 "It's not reality": Inspired by Shawn Achor, "The Secret to Better Work," filmed May 2011 in Bloomington, IN, TEDxBloomington video, 6:05, https://www.ted.com/talks/shawn_achor_the_happy _secret_to_better_work/transcript?language=en#t-366525.

20 "internal locus of control": Alexandra Stocks, Kurt A. April, and Nandani Lynton, "Locus of Control and Subjective Well-Being—A Cross-Cultural Study," *Problems and Perspectives in Management* 10, no. 1 (2012): 18.

22 "Squirrel Strategy": Erik Weihenmayer and Buddy Levy, *No Barriers:*

A Blind Man's Journey to Kayak the Grand Canyon (New York: Thomas Dunne Books, 2017).

23 "push back against the rules": Lauren R. Bangerter et al., "Honoring the Everyday Preferences of Nursing Home Residents: Perceived Choice and Satisfaction with Care," *Gerontologist* 57, no. 3 (June 2017): 479–86, https://doi.org/10.1093/geront/gnv697.

23 "more successful when reentering society": "Why Prison Education?," Prison Studies Project, accessed February 11, 2019, http://prisonstudiesproject.org/why-prison-education-programs/.

24 "current life span": "Average Life Expectancy in North America for Those Born in 2018, by Gender and Region," Statista, August 2018, https://www.statista.com/statistics/274513/life-expectancy-in-north-america/.

34 "I wish I'd . . .": Bronnie Ware, *The Top Five Regrets of the Dying: A Life Transformed by the Dearly Departing* (Carlsbad, CA: Hay House, 2011).

CHAPTER 3: DISCOVER YOUR NORTH STAR

38 "Merchant of Death Is Dead": Ken Makovsky, "Nobel: How He Built His Reputation," *Forbes*, November 7, 2011, https://www.forbes.com/sites/kenmakovsky/2011/11/07/nobel-how-he-built-his-reputation/#5f3691e72d36.

42 "Human beings are works in progress": Daniel Gilbert, "The Psychology of the Future Self," TED Talk, video, 6:45, March 2014, https://www.ted.com/talks/dan_gilbert_you_are_always_changing?language=en.

43 "Amazon": Lawrence Gregory, "Amazon.com Inc.'s Mission Statement & Vision Statement (An Analysis)," Panmore Institute, updated February 13, 2019, http://panmore.com/amazon-com-inc-vision-statement-mission-statement-analysis.

43 "Nike": Nathaniel Smithson, "Nike Inc.'s Mission Statement & Vision Statement (An Analysis)," Panmore Institute, updated February 14, 2019, http://panmore.com/nike-inc-vision-statement-mission-statement.

43 "PBS": "Support PBS," PBS, http://www.pbs.org/about/support-pbs/.

44 "To be a teacher": Oprah Winfrey, "Every Person Has a Purpose," Oprah.com, accessed June 28, 2019, https://www.oprah.com/spirit /how-oprah-winfrey-found-her-purpose.

44 "To have fun": Drew Hendricks, "Personal Mission Statement of 13 CEOs and Lessons You Need to Learn," *Forbes*, November 10, 2014, https://www.forbes.com/sites/drewhendricks/2014/11/10/personal -mission-statement-of-14-ceos-and-lessons-you-need-to-learn /#d4e03ed1e5ea.

45 "I use my humor": Post from author's private Facebook group, October 28, 2017.

46 "Make-A-Wish": "Make-A-Wish Eastern North Carolina," GuideStar, https://www.guidestar.org/profile/58–1792140.

46 "Avon": "Our Values," Avon.com, https://www.avonworldwide.com /about-us/our-values.

46 "ASPCA": "ASPCA Policy and Position Statements," ASPCA, https ://www.aspca.org/about-us/aspca-policy-and-position-statements/vision.

48 "Smithsonian": "About the Museum," Smithsonian Museum of Natural History, https://web.archive.org/web/20181024175227 /https://naturalhistory.si.edu/about/mission.htm.

48 "Adidas": "Vision and Values," Adidas Group, http://sustainabilityreport .adidas-group.com/en/SER2007/b/b_1.asp.

48 "Adobe": "Adobe Fast Facts," Adobe, https://www.adobe.com/about -adobe/fast-facts.html.

51 "Remembering that I'll be dead soon": Steve Jobs (commencement address, Stanford University, Stanford, CA, June 12, 2005), prepared text available at "'You've Got to Find What You Love,' Jobs Says," *Stanford Report*, June 14, 2005, https://news.stanford.edu/news/2005 /june15/jobs-061505.html.

CHAPTER 4: CLARIFY FOCUS

57 "we receive approximately 11 million": David DiSalvo, "Your Brain Sees Even When You Don't," *Forbes*, June 22, 2013, https://www

.forbes.com/sites/daviddisalvo/2013/06/22/your-brain-sees-even
-when-you-dont/#51e0c7f1116a.

57 "Just as snow blindness refers": Charles Duhigg, *Smarter Faster Better: The Transformative Power of Real Productivity* (New York: Random House, 2016), 243.

57 "processing a few snowflakes": Shawn Achor, "The Happiness Advantage" (Women's Presidents Organization, Orlando, FL, May 5, 2017).

58 "he was able to ignite": Ingvar nord (username), "Archimedes Mirrors, Modern Research," Ancient Origins forums, December 19, 2017, https://www.ancient-origins.net/forum/archimedes-mirrors-modern -research-009308.

58 "Concentrate all your thought": Alexander Graham Bell, interviewed in Orison Swett Marden, *How They Succeeded: Life Stories of Successful Men Told by Themselves* (Boston: Lothrop Publishing, 1901), 34.

59 "the real success story was in the 3 percent": Mark H. McCormack, *What They Don't Teach You at Harvard Business School: Notes from a Street-Smart Executive* (New York: Bantam, 1984).

59 "If you aim at nothing": Quoted at Tom Ziglar, "If You Aim at Nothing . . . ," Ziglar.com, accessed February 18, 2019, https://www .ziglar.com/articles/if-you-aim-at-nothing-2/.

61 "one in three people claimed": Karen Renaud, Judith Ramsay, and Mario Hair, "'You've Got E-Mail!' . . . Shall I Deal with It Now? Electronic Mail from the Recipient's Perspective," *International Journal of Human–Computer Interaction* 21, no. 3 (2006): 313–32, https ://doi.org/10.1207/s15327590ijhc2103_3.

61 "today's digital world where": Eric Barker, "This Is How to Increase Your Attention Span: 5 Secrets from Neuroscience," Ladders, March 31, 2018, https://www.theladders.com/career-advice/this-is -how-to-increase-your-attention-span-5-secrets-from-neuroscience.

61 "researchers estimate that workers are interrupted": Bob Sullivan and Hugh Thompson, "Brain, Interrupted," *New York Times*, May 3,

2013, https://www.nytimes.com/2013/05/05/opinion/sunday/a
-focus-on-distraction.html.

66 "Because people have access": Personal conversation with author, April 24, 2018.

67 "the clearer and more respected our boundaries": Brené Brown, *Braving the Wilderness: The Quest for True Belonging and the Courage to Stand Alone* (New York: Random House, 2017), 70–71.

CHAPTER 5: CLARIFY TIME

71 "Scientists have discovered that when we multitask": Susan Weinschenk, "The True Cost of Multi-Tasking," *Psychology Today*, September 18, 2012, https://www.psychologytoday.com/us/blog/brain-wise/201209 /the-true-cost-multi-tasking.

71 "When we multitask": Larry Kim, "Multitasking Is Killing Your Brain," *Inc.*, July 15, 2015, https://www.inc.com/larry-kim/why-multi -tasking-is-killing-your-brain.html.

72 "The better someone believed she was at multitasking": Maria Konnikova, "Multitask Masters," *New Yorker*, May 7, 2014, https ://www.newyorker.com/science/maria-konnikova/multitask-masters.

73 "You've probably heard of your circadian rhythm": "Circadian Rhythm," ScienceDaily, accessed February 12, 2019, https://www .sciencedaily.com/terms/circadian_rhythm.htm.

73 "There is the in-breath": Quoted in Brown, *Braving the Wilderness*, 148.

75 "Workers who put in seventy hours": Bob Sullivan, "Memo to Work Martyrs: Long Hours Make You Less Productive," CNBC, January 26, 2015, https://www.cnbc.com/2015/01/26/working-more-than-50 -hours-makes-you-less-productive.html.

75 "In 1914 Henry Ford": Sara Robinson, "Bring Back the 40-Hour Work Week," Salon, March 14, 2012, https://www.salon.com/2012 /03/14/bring_back_the_40_hour_work_week/.

76 "I am a night owl": Post from author's private Facebook group, March 28, 2018.

76 "Writing triggers the reticular activating system": Henriette Anne

Klauser, *Write It Down, Make It Happen: Knowing What You Want— And Getting It!* (New York: Scribner, 2000), chap. 1.

76 "A joint study between Princeton and UCLA": Wray Herbert, "Ink on Paper: Some Notes on Note Taking*," Association for Psychological Science, January 28, 2014, https://www.psychologicalscience.org/news /were-only-human/ink-on-paper-some-notes-on-note-taking.html.

79 "Warren Buffett attributes 90 percent": Mary Buffett and David Clark, *The Tao of Warren Buffett* (New York: Scribner, 2006), 68.

79 "work expands so as to fill": *Merriam-Webster Dictionary*, s.v. "Parkinson's Law," accessed February 12, 2019, https://www.merriam -webster.com/dictionary/Parkinson%27s%20Law.

80 "When you're up against a wall": Marie Forleo, "How to Double Your Results and Actually Work Less," MarieForleo.com, July 2010, https://www.marieforleo.com/2010/07/double-results-work /#ixzz3WHqTDeYf.

81 "Too often our work": Thomas S. Greenspon, "'Healthy Perfectionism' Is an Oxymoron: Reflections on the Psychology of Perfectionism and the Sociology of Science," *Journal of Advanced Academics* 11, no. 4 (2000): 197–208, https://doi.org/10.4219/jsge-2000-631.

CHAPTER 6: CLARIFY ENERGY

83 "It's Linus when his blanket": Quoted in William Bridges, *Managing Transitions: Making the Most of Change* (Cambridge, MA: Da Capo Press, 2009), chap. 4.

84 "It's not enough to be busy": Henry David Thoreau to Harrison Gray Otis Blake, November 16, 1857, in *The Correspondence of Henry David Thoreau*, ed. Walter Harding and Carl Bode (Washington Square: New York University Press, 1958), 496. Access provided through the Walden Woods Project, https://www.walden.org/our -collections/the-correspondence-of-henry-david-thoreau/.

84 "We are using our lists": Kat McGowan, "Is the To-Do List Doing You In?," *Psychology Today*, December 7, 2005, https://www .psychologytoday.com/us/articles/200512/is-the-do-list-doing-you-in.

85 "by the end of the average workday": "New LinkedIn Research Reveals Which Professionals Conquer Their To-Do Lists," LinkedIn News, May 12, 2012, http://www.linkedinnews.org/new-linkedin-research -reveals-which-professionals-conquer-their-to-do-lists/.

91 "She seemed to love her newfound motherhood": Post from author's private Facebook group, November 2, 2017.

93 "Herb Kelleher, former CEO of Southwest Airlines": Jeff Haden, "Want to Accomplish More in Less Time? 9 Things the Most Effective People Always Do," *Inc.*, July 31, 2017, https://www.inc.com/jeff -haden/want-to-accomplish-more-in-less-time-9-things-the-.html.

93 "Southwest's mission was to": "Purpose, Vision, Values, and Mission," Southwest, accessed February 13, 2019, http://investors.southwest. com/our-company/purpose-vision-values-and-mission.

94 "I always knew I'd be a millionaire": Quoted in George B., "Revealed: Oprah Predicted She'll Be a Millionaire by 30," EliteSavvy, March 17, 2017, http://elitesavvy.com/2017/03/17/revealed-oprah-predicted -shell-millionaire-30/.

94 "The big secret in life": George B., "Revealed: Oprah Predicted."

95 "I don't read work emails after 7 p.m.": J. J. McCorvey, "Shonda Rimes' Rules of Work: 'Come into My Office with a Solution, Not a Problem,'" *Fast Company*, November 27, 2016, https://www .fastcompany.com/3065423/shonda-rhimes.

95 "If the thing that ABC is paying me": McCorvey, "Shonda Rimes' Rules."

95 "It suddenly occurred to me": "Shonda Rhimes on Running 3 Hit Shows and the Limits of Network TV," NPR, November 11, 2015, https://www.npr.org/2015/11/11/455594842/shonda-rhimes-on -running-three-hit-shows-and-the-limits-of-network-tv.

96 "The difference between successful people": Marcel Schwantes, "Warren Buffett Says This 1 Simple Habit Separates Successful People from Everyone Else," *Inc.*, January 18, 2018, https://www.inc.com /marcel-schwantes/warren-buffett-says-this-is-1-simple-habit-that -separates-successful-people-from-everyone-else.html.

96 "Remember, focused energy": Marguerite Ward, "How to Follow Warren Buffett's No. 1 for Success," CNBC, June 23, 2017, https ://www.cnbc.com/2017/06/23/berkshire-hathaways-warren-buffett -shares-his-top-rule-for-success.html.

98 "I would donate it.": From a personal interview with the author, March 28, 2018.

CHAPTER 7: SIMPLIFY SYSTEMS

105 "Happiness increases if we view our tasks": Christopher Bergland, "The Secret to Achieving a Big Goal Is . . . ," *Psychology Today*, May 30, 2013, https://www.psychologytoday.com/us/blog/the -athletes-way/201305/the-secret-achieving-big-goal-is.

108 "Your brain takes up a mere 2 percent": Ferris Jabr, "Does Thinking Really Hard Burn Calories?," *Scientific American*, July 18, 2012, https://www.scientificamerican.com/article/thinking-hard-calories/.

109 "Our perfectly rational brain loses": John Tierney, "Do You Suffer from Decision Fatigue?," *New York Times Magazine*, August 17, 2011, https://www.nytimes.com/2011/08/21/magazine/do-you-suffer-from -decision-fatigue.html.

109 "Knowing the right choice takes brainpower": Jonah Lehrer, "Blame It on the Brain," *Wall Street Journal*, December 26, 2009, https://www.wsj .com/articles/SB10001424052748703478704574612052322122442.

110 "Since they involve my family": Quoted from a personal assessment from one of the author's online courses.

110 "We think all habits are bad": David T. Neal, Wendy Wood, and Jeffrey M. Quinn, "Habits—A Repeat Performance," *Current Directions in Psychological Science* 15, no. 4 (2006): 198–202, https://doi.org /10.1111/j.1467-8721.2006.00435.x.

111 "the brain starts working less and less": Charles Duhigg, *The Power of Habit: Why We Do What We Do in Life and Business* (New York: Random House, 2012).

112 "He believes there are five cues": Duhigg, 283.

113 "When we try to form and keep habits": Gretchen Rubin, "Which of These 10 Categories of Loopholes Do You Invoke?," *Gretchen Rubin* (blog), February 5, 2014, https://gretchenrubin.com/2014/02/which -of-these-10-categories-of-loopholes-do-you-invoke/.

113 "I have felt for a while that life was controlling me": Post from author's private Facebook group, April 9, 2018.

113 "Most people have a sweet spot": Phillippa Lally et al., "How Are Habits Formed: Modelling Habit Formation in the Real World," *European Journal of Social Psychology* 40, no. 6 (October 2010): 998–1009, https://doi.org/10.1002/ejsp.674.

114 "Once the habit becomes set": Courtney Humphries, "Why We Do What We Do," *MIT Technology Review*, December 17, 2013, https://www.technologyreview.com/s/522521/why-we-do-what -we-do/.

115 "Gretchen Rubin would define": Rubin, "Which of These 10 Categories of Loopholes Do You Invoke?"

CHAPTER 8: SIMPLIFY ROUTINES

119 "But in 1983 physicist Lorne Whitehead": Lorne A. Whitehead, "Domino 'Chain Reaction,'" *American Journal of Physics* 51, no. 82 (1983): 182.

120 "Our bodies are made up of almost 60 percent water": Waseem Abbasi, "Why You Should Drink Water First Thing Every Day," *USA Today*, March 14, 2017, https://www.usatoday.com/story/news /nation-now/2017/03/14/why-you-should-drink-water-first-thing -every-day/99123938/.

122 "I just want to feel like I [do] something meaningful": Post from author's private Facebook group, April 10, 2018.

124 "Ma said each day had its own proper work": Laura Ingalls Wilder, *Little House in the Big Woods* (New York: HarperTrophy, 1971), 29.

127 "I love that automations clear space in my mind": From a personal interview with the author, June 6, 2018.

CHAPTER 9: SIMPLIFY STRUCTURE

131 "*Hustle* is just a more aggressive word": *Merriam-Webster Dictionary*, s.v. "hustle," accessed February 14, 2019, https://www.merriam -webster.com/dictionary/hustle.

132 "Because when we feel in control": G. R. Hockey and F. Earle, "Control over the Scheduling of Simulated Office Work Reduces the Impact of Workload on Mental Fatigue and Task Performance," *Journal of Experimental Psychology: Applied* 12, no. 1 (March 2006): 50–65, https://doi.org/10.1037/1076-898X.12.1.50.

133 "Studies show that our work suffers": Sian L. Beilock and Thomas H. Carr, "When High-Powered People Fail: Working Memory and 'Choking Under Pressure' in Math," *Psychological Science* 16, no.2 (2005): 101–105, https://doi.org/10.1111/j.0956-7976.2005 .00789.x.

134 "I love planning at the beginning": From post in author's private Facebook group, June 21, 2018.

136 "I use the focus [area]": From a post in author's private Facebook group, March 27, 2018.

137 "If you don't prioritize your life": Greg McKeown, *Essentialism: The Disciplined Pursuit of Less* (New York: Crown Business, 2014), 235.

138 "I accomplish a lot more tasks": From a post in a private Facebook group, August 1, 2017.

139 "It takes over twenty minutes for the brain": Gloria Mark, Daniela Gudith, and Ulrich Klocke, "The Cost of Interrupted Work: More Speed and Stress," *Proceedings of the SIGCHI Conference on Human Factors in Computing Systems* (2008): 107–10, https://doi.org/10.1145 /1357054.1357072.

142 "As long as you can start": Ernest Hemingway, interviewed by George Plimpton in *Ernest Hemingway's The Sun Also Rises: A Casebook*, ed. Linda Wagner-Martin (New York: Oxford University Press, 2002), 19, 21.

143 "In fact, one study found": Leigh Buchanan, "Inside the Psychology of Productivity," *Inc.*, February 18, 2015, https://www.inc.com /magazine/201503/leigh-buchanan/the-psychology-of-productivity.html.

144 "According to happiness expert Shawn Achor": Brigid Schulte, "Do These Exercises for Two Minutes a Day and You'll Immediately Feel Happier, Researchers Say," *Washington Post*, June 29, 2015, https ://www.washingtonpost.com/news/inspired-life/wp/2015/06/29/do -these-exercises-for-two-minutes-a-day-and-youll-immediately-feel -happier-researchers-say/?noredirect=on&utm_term=.2d73a0c265fc.

CHAPTER 10: HARMONIZE WHITESPACE

149 "Any given 24 hours": Laura Vanderkam, *I Know How She Does It: How Successful Women Make the Most of Their Time* (New York: Portfolio/Penguin, 2015), 72.

151 "That's how Stephen King reads": Elle Kaplan, "How to Read (a Lot) More Books This Year, According to Harvard Research," *Medium*, March 27, 2017, https://medium.com/the-mission/how-to-read-a-lot -more-books-this-year-according-to-harvard-research-e1dfc55e0b9f.

153 "It wasn't until a recent expedition": *Jaws of the Deep*, TV documentary, directed by Nick Stringer, aired July 27, 2016, on Discovery Channel's 2016 *Shark Week*. Footage re-aired for *Shark Week 2018* as part of "Sharkcam Strikes Back."

155 "Recent studies show the average person": David Cohen, "How Much Time Will the Average Person Spend on Social Media During Their Life? (Infographic)," *Adweek*, March 22, 2017, https://www.adweek .com/digital/mediakix-time-spent-social-media-infographic/.

156 "My boundaries for self-care": From a post in author's private Facebook group, April 6, 2018.

157 "Woo Hoo! Today I sent the kids": From a post in author's private Facebook group, April 13, 2018.

159 "To bring out the best in others": John C. Maxwell, *Developing the Leader Within You 2.0* (Nashville: HarperCollins Leadership, 2018), 154.

159 "increases our problem-solving abilities": J. David Creswell et al., "Self-Affirmation Improves Problem-Solving Under Stress," *PLoS ONE* 8, no. 5 (2013): e62593, https://doi.org/10.1371/journal .pone.0062593.

159 "helps us bounce back": Marina Krakovsky, "Self-Compassion Fosters Mental Health," *Scientific American*, July 1, 2012, https://www .scientificamerican.com/article/self-compassion-fosters-mental-health/.

159 "evidence affirming it even increases": Juliana G. Breines and Serena Chen, "Self-Compassion Increases Self-Improvement Motivation," *Personality and Social Psychology Bulletin* 38, no. 9 (2012): 1133–43, https://doi.org/10.1177/0146167212445599.

159 "In other words, when we practice self-compassion": University of Hertfordshire, "Self-Acceptance Could Be the Key to a Happier Life, Yet It's the Happy Habit Many People Practice the Least," ScienceDaily, March 7, 2014, www.sciencedaily.com/releases/2014 /03/140307111016.htm.

160 "It seems counterintuitive, but space allows": University of Illinois at Urbana–Champaign, "Brief Diversions Vastly Improve Focus, Researchers Find," ScienceDaily, February 8, 2011, https://www .sciencedaily.com/releases/2011/02/110208131529.htm.

160 "We have a thousand words for busy": At the time of this writing, the antonyms to busy listed by M-W include *idle, inactive, unbusy, unemployed, unoccupied*, per Merriam-Webster, https://www.merriam -webster.com/dictionary/busy.

CHAPTER 11: HARMONIZE YOUR YES

166 "I got to the end of the year": From a personal interview with the author, July 17, 2018.

169 "None of it was random": From a personal phone interview with the author, July 17, 2018.

173 "We must not confuse the command": Lysa TerKeurst, *The Best Yes: Making Wise Decisions in the Midst of Endless Demands* (Nashville: Thomas Nelson, 2014), 5.

CHAPTER 12: HARMONIZE LIFE

180 "Because of our selective attention": Josh Hrala, "You Know How When You Learn a New Word, You See It Everywhere? Science Knows

Why," Science Alert, March 24, 2016, https://www.sciencealert.com /you-know-how-when-you-learn-a-new-word-you-see-it-everywhere -here-s-why.

182 "They tell you to develop a thick skin": Brené Brown, "Courage and Power from Pain: An Interview with Viola Davis," *Brené Brown* (blog), May 9, 2018, https://brenebrown.com/blog/2018/05/09/courage -power-pain-interview-viola-davis/.

185 "If I spent all my time in the mountains": From a personal interview with the author in Buena Vista, Colorado, July 12, 2018.

CONCLUSION

193 "fake it till [we] become it": Amy Cuddy, "Your Body Language May Shape Who You Are," TED Talk, video, 20:56, June 2012, https ://www.ted.com/talks/amy_cuddy_your_body_language_shapes_who _you_are.

ABOUT THE AUTHOR

TONYA DALTON is a wife, mother, entrepreneur, and recovering perfectionist. She is the CEO and founder of inkWELL Press Productivity Co., a multimillion-dollar company focused on helping women live productive lives centered around their priorities. Whether listening to Tonya's weekly podcast, hearing her speak, or visiting her social media feed, you'll walk away with real, actionable advice on living your best life at home and at work.

Tonya has been featured on Fast Company, *Inc.*, Entrepreneur, Real Simple, Elite Daily, Today.com, and Buzzfeed, among other places. She has been named the North Carolina Entrepreneur to Watch and was awarded the Enterprising Woman of the Year for 2019.

Those who know her best describe Tonya simply as a mom who loves her family fiercely, isn't afraid to make a fool of herself, and wants nothing more than for you to stop overthinking and start working towards the life you really want.

———

If you enjoyed *The Joy of Missing Out*, make sure to connect with Tonya at TonyaDalton.com or on social media where she often posts pictures of her family and daily life.

YOU WANT MORE THAN A PRODUCTIVE LIFE, YOU
WANT THE BEAUTIFUL LIFE YOU DESERVE.

It's not just another Facebook group...

Tonya's free online community is an encouraging and interactive
space for anyone who wants to gain support in their journey toward
peak productivity.

From monthly challenges that are achievable and fun, to discussions
on your personal priorities and overall happiness, Tonya creates a
helpful and supportive experience for all members of her community.

Visit TONYADALTON.COM/GROUP to join!

liveWELL METHOD™
Course

A groundbreaking course redefining productivity for the modern woman.
We all have the same 168 hours in our week. The difference is how you prioritize your time, energy, and focus in a way that works for you.

In Tonya's 4-module online course, you'll dive even deeper into each of the sections: Discovery, Clarity, Simplicity, and Harmony, to create your own personalized productivity systems.

During the liveWELL Method, you'll bring the joy of missing out into your own life with this immersive experience as Tonya guides you through conquering overwhelm, achieving harmony, and creating a life you love.

Go to **TONYADALTON.COM/COURSE** *to enroll!*

PRODUCTIVITY PARADOX.
Podcast

Tonya's weekly podcast, *Productivity Paradox*, is packed full of actionable strategies and exercises that are achievable and effective. In each 20-minute episode, Tonya walks you through how to create a life centered around your priorities.

From time management, streamlining, prioritizing and planning, *Productivity Paradox* is ideal for anyone who wants to create life-changing results in their personal life, relationships, or business.

Visit **TONYADALTON.COM/PODCAST** *to start listening!*